AFTER ORLANDO

(The Pulse Nightclub Plays)

An international theatre action in response to the Pulse nightclub shooting

edited by Caridad Svich

NoPassport Press

Dreaming the Americas Series

After Orlando.

(The Pulse Nightclub Plays)

2024.

All rights Reserved.

All authors retain individual copyright to their work.

All performance rights queries go to individual authors and/or their representatives.

NoPassport Press

Dreaming the Americas Series

PO Box 1786

South Gate, CA 90280 USA.

https://www.nopassport.org

ISBN: 978-1-300-74757-4

The Authors and Their Plays

Oladipo Agboluaje, *Ice Cream*, 9

Asiimwe Deborah Kawe: *Maybe S/he*, 16

Jaisey Bates: *They Were Dancing*, 25

Migdalia Cruz: *Orlando 2:02 AM*, 37

Nathan Alan Davis: *The Gun Collector*, 44

Georgina Escobar, *Matted*, 52

Lindsey Ferrentino, *Orlando monologue*, 65

Andy Field: *Pistols*, 75

Ryan Gielen: *The Healing Power of Bright Colors*, 78

Jacqueline Goldfinger: *Baby Sister*, 84

Garret Jon Groenveld: *He Comes Up Behind Me*, 94

C. Julian Jiménez: *We are Molecules*, 99

Alexander Kveton: *Ally*, 107

Deb Laufer: *Everybody gets a stick*, 113

E.M. Lewis, *And Then the Music…*, 119

Joan Lipkin, *Our Friends*, 127

Anders Lustgarten: *The Human Traces*, 139

Jennifer Maisel: *Gone Silent*, 146

Jeff McMahon: *Ob(scene)*, 155

Oliver Mayer: *After Orlando*, 161

Ryan Oliveira: *The life and times of a gay club*, 166

Matthew Paul Olmos: *The Bigger Picture*, 176

Giovanni Ortega: *The Sea*, 182

Katie Pearl: *Today is a Good Day*, 196

Brian Quijada: *Til the DJ Quits Playing*, 202

Sung Rno: *Sauce*, 208

Elaine Romero: *Orlando*, 217

Ian Rowlands: *Dance On*, 230

Riti Sachdeva: *AFTER (a kinda litany or something)*, 239

Madeline Sayet, *Could You Love Me?*, 244

Lisa Schlesinger: *Before. Before. After*, 250

dave solomon: *Light*, 259

Saviana Stanescu, *Stroboscope*, 263

Ken Urban: *Claim*, 270

After Orlando was an international theatre action conceived in summer of 2016 by Missing Bolts Productions (Blair Baker and Zac Kline) and NoPassport theatre alliance (Caridad Svich, founder).

The action was comprised of upwards of 75 short plays written in response to the Pulse nightclub shooting in Orlando, Florida on June 12, 2016.

On that day, 29-year-old Omar Mateen shot and killed 49 people and wounded 53 more people at Pulse, an LGBTQIA nightclub in Orlando, Florida (USA). On that night Pulse was hosting a "Latin Night" and most of the victims of the mass shooting were Latine.

The plays written for this theatre action, of which the ones in this book are only a part, were read script in hand at theatres and community centres across the US and abroad in the months following the aftermath of the mass shooting, including a special event at Orlando Shakespeare Festival on November 5, 2016, where Caridad Svich gave the keynote address "The Dreaming: on making art in the aftermath of tragedy."

Four special benefit readings directed by Wendy Goldberg were presented at DR2 in

New York City on November 13, 20, December 4 and 11, 2016 with proceeds going to Pulse of Orlando Fund for victims and survivors of the attack.

At the time of the theatre action, Baker and Kline stated: 'As theatre-makers, we have the ability to bring together many singular unique voices toward a common goal. We feel it necessary to give artists a place to respond to the tragedy in Orlando and the current state of the world to share our grief, anger, and our hope and desire to combat the violence we are now living with daily." Caridad Svich remarked also at the time "Making some healing art, some fiery art, some work that just says we can rise from and through collective mourning."

This collection is comprised of a selection of the plays written for the theatre action and are dedicated to the memory of the 49 people lost on that day, to the 53 wounded, and to all the survivors of the tragedy and their loved ones in the LGBTQIA community.

Net proceeds of any sales of this book will be donated by NoPassport Press to the Orlando United Pulse Memorial Fund, established in spring of 2024, which exists within the city's Strength Orlando nonprofit.

Ice Cream

By Oladipo Agboluaje

Oladipo Agboluaje is a British-Nigerian playwright. He was born in Hackney and educated in Britain and Nigeria. He has served on the boards of Oval House (now Brixton House) and Soho Theatre. He was the 2019 writer in residence of the National Theatre in London.

CHARACTERS

Ayeesha, 7

Daddy One

Daddy Two

AYEESHA, DADDY ONE and DADDY TWO, in a car, driving on the motorway.

AYEESHA: Daddy One says, 'what do you want to be when you grow up?' Daddy Two says, 'don't answer that Ayeesha! You've got plenty of time to decide when you're older.' But I know what I'm going to be – I am going to be the first black president of the United States of America!

DADDY ONE: Female black president.

AYEESHA: I am going to be the first black *female* president of the United States of America!

DADDY TWO: You hear that? Our baby is going to become president.

AYEESHA: I'm going to make America great again!

DADDY TWO: Oh, OK...

DADDY ONE nudges DADDY TWO.

DADDY TWO: Yeah! You go for it, girl. Just don't grow up too soon.

AYEESHA: I promise, Daddy Two.

DADDY ONE: Don't listen to Daddy Two, Ayeesha baby. You grow up as fast as you want.

DADDY TWO: Not if you don't want to. Your childhood is precious…

DADDY ONE and DADDY TWO argue.

AYEESHA: This is how they argue because Daddy One always thinks of stuff like college tuition, and Daddy Two always thinks of stuff like my next hair makeover. I bury my giggles in Coco's fluffy chest. Daddy One thinks I'm too old to be playing with Coco but Daddy Two says I'll grow out of teddy bears when boys or girls come knocking and that Daddy One didn't stop wetting the bed until he was fourteen. And Daddy One says I shouldn't laugh because I wet the bed twice this week, and he was going to call the *Guinness Book of Records* because I'm the first child in the whole wide world to wet the bed twice in one week. And I scream when Daddy One asks Daddy Two to pass him his cell phone.

DADDY TWO: You say when you're hungry, baby.

AYEESHA: You've asked me twice already, Daddy Two.

DADDY TWO: That's because Daddy Two loves you.

AYEESHA: I know, Daddy Two.

DADDY ONE: (*Pretend serious.*) So you DO love Daddy Two more than you love me!

AYEESHA: I don't!

DADDY ONE: Yes, you do!

AYEESHA: No, I don't! I love you both the same.

And I say I want ice cream. And Daddy One says ice cream is not food and Daddy Two says, don't worry baby, we'll get you some at the next stop. And because Daddy One is bad at playing bad cop, I'm dancing in my seat because I can see my face covered in chocolate and strawberry. And Daddy Two starts talking about the couple three stops back at the Walmart who asked what they were doing with a child and that they were disgusting because they touched hands. I asked Daddy Two what does disgusting mean and he said he'd tell me later and I didn't bug him like I do when I'm curious because he looked hurt, so I kind of knew what it meant, like something bad, and I was sorry that I had to go toilet because before that they were holding my hands. And I was going to ask him what disgusting meant but he had that hurt look on his face again. And those nasty people said they were going to call the police and Daddy One said I am the police even though he is so bad at playing bad cop. And I see Daddy One make the 'not in front of Ayeesha' eyes. And I know it's something really, really bad because that's the only time they make those eyes, like when Christy, my babysitter died or when I asked Daddy One and Daddy Two if they really were faggots because my classmate Henry told the whole class they were. But Daddy Two is worried because he saw the woman talking on her cell phone and looking at our car. And Daddy One says –

DADDY ONE: Come on, what are you worrying for?

AYEESHA: And Daddy Two says a black cop out of uniform is just a black man something target something like every other something, and I can't hear clearly because he's mumbling because he doesn't want me to hear. But I stop worrying because Daddy One has used his phone to find the nearest ice cream store and it's nearby and he's asking me what flavor I want and I say chocolate and strawberry and he knows it's my favorite so why was he asking. And he says, there goes your college tuition. It's Daddy Two who tells us that a passing police car has made a U-turn and is following us. And Daddy One says we should stay calm because we haven't done anything wrong. And the police siren goes off and Daddy Two is telling Daddy One to pull over and Daddy One tells Daddy Two not to scare me. But I'm not afraid because at school I saw a video on the internet where cops like Daddy One give out free ice cream. And I was telling Daddy One to pull over so we could get the free ice cream and he could save money for my college tuition. But Daddy One says it's safer if he drives into the car park and that's where he parks. Daddy One asks the officer what's the problem? I want to ask the officer if he's got chocolate and strawberry but the way he asks for Daddy One's license and registration is like Daddy One did something wrong. Daddy Two tells Daddy One to show the officer his badge but Daddy One says we've done nothing wrong. The officer tells Daddy One that he was texting on his phone and asks again for Daddy One's license and registration, and he is looking at me funny. And Daddy One is asking the officer why he is looking at me like that, and the officer asks me who I am, and Daddy One says it was that couple back at the Walmart that reported us, that's why he stopped us. And Daddy Two is scared like I've never seen him before and he reaches into Daddy One's pocket, saying officer hold on and the officer is shouting and reaching for his gun, and Daddy One is shouting and suddenly Daddy Two and Daddy One are covered in strawberry. And now only the officer is shouting because Daddy One and Daddy Two are no longer talking. And I start to cry, because the noise before Daddy One and Daddy Two fell and lay on each other like they do on the sofa is very loud, and I think the officer is going to make me go quiet too because he is pointing his gun at me. And I hide my face in Coco's chest and I scream.

The End

Maybe S/he....

By Asiimwe Deborah Kawe

Asiimwe Deborah Kawe is an award-winning playwright, producer and performer. She is the founding Producing Artistic Director of Tebere Arts Foundation and the Artistic Director of the Kampala International Theatre Festival. Ms. Kawe worked with the Sundance Theatre Program, leading the East Africa initiative for six years. She received a B. A. in Theatre from Makerere University and an M.F.A. in Writing for Performance from the California Institute of the Arts.

Rights: C/O Masterly Book and Stationery Point, Plot 59/61 Kampala Road, P.O Box 25565, Kampala-Uganda, Tel. +256783545504, Email: dasiimwe@gmail.com

*

It was another day, a new day. A day that held many joys and promises. A day she was going to fall in love. A day he was going to make up with his friend….

It was another day, it was a new day.

Maybe, she woke up with a leap in her feet. He probably woke up with a smile on his face. They woke up looking forward to making the most of the day….

It was another day, it was a new day.

Maybe, while eating his breakfast, he called his mother and told her how much he missed her. How much he loved her. Maybe, she called her brother and told him to work hard at his grades, reminded him how much she believed in him….

It was another day, it was a new day.

Maybe, her Dad called her and wanted her to have dinner with the family, but she couldn't because she had made plans to hang out with her friends. Maybe, his colleague at work called him to ask if he could cover for him that evening, but he couldn't because he already made plans for the evening….

It was another day, it was a new day.

Maybe, she was feeling a little under the weather and wanted to stay indoors, but one phone call from someone she loved dearly changed it all, and she decided to go hang out with her. Maybe, he had planned to work another shift to send extra bucks back to his grandmother in his home country, but one phone call made him change his mind. He would go dancing instead….

It was another day, it was a new day.

Maybe, she had an amazing work out, the kind she had never had before and she promised herself to journal about it later that night. Maybe, that was the night he was going to close that business deal, and he was looking forward to it….

It was another day, it was a new day.

Maybe, they couldn't wait for the evening to come, maybe they could not wait to get on the road. As they left work, as they took a shower, dried their hair, dressed up, applied make up, took the first step out of the house with a hop in their feet, with a smile on their face, with joy inside them, and a laughter in their heart….

It was another day, it was a new day.

Maybe, at the entrance of the club, some of them were simply let in because they were familiar faces, maybe others were asked for their IDs, maybe others were asked to step aside because they looked too young to be in a night club. They probably laughed and giggled as they fetched more evidence to prove that their looks had nothing to do with their age….

It was another day, it was a new day.

Maybe, he was going to start on a new job in a week's time, or a month's time. Maybe, she was going to be promoted in a few days. Maybe, they were going to be parents. Maybe, they had promised to visit friends in another state….

It was another day, it was a new day.

In a different space, in a different time, in a different state of mind…

They wake up.

They plot.

They lay their strategies.

They obtain their lethal.

They pay for the venom.

Ready to bite

Ready to sting

Ready to inject

Ready to strike

They move.

In different states across this land, in different towns, urban and rural, on our college and school campuses, in homes and on our streets, in every corner across this planet, someone, young, old wakes up to a new day, to new promises, to new dreams, to new aspirations, then that sound, the sound….

The sound of

Poo poo

Crack, Crack, Crakkkkkk

Kkkkkkkk, Kkkkkkk

Phrrr, phrrr, phrrr

Phwrrrr, Phwrrr

That sound

and it is all over.

In the news, on our screens, in our cars, on our phones the story unfolds

All. Over. Again.

Just like:

Yesterday's story

The other day's story

Last week's story

Last month's story

Last year's story

Several year's story

                           We look on, we
                    pray, we sob, we weep, we
                           fret,

We wonder….

               when will it be me?

We wonder…

Where will I be?

In a Church?

                        In a movie theatre?

            At School?

On a bus?

            On a train?

At some airport?

            We mourn for her

            We mourn for him

                        We mourn
                        for them

And tomorrow, it is again yesterday's story.

It does not stop

We sigh when will it ever stop,

We fear it will not stop

Yet we know, it could stop

We know, it is possible to stop

Tomorrow is another day

What story do we want to write?

What do we want to read?

What story do we want to watch?

What story do we want to wake up to?

What story do we want to sleep on?

What story do we want our children hold?

This story, the story we have fed on for decades

This story we fear to see again

This story we can't bear to hear again

This story that has left families shuttered

This story that is unspeakable

This story can change

This story needs to change

This story must change…..

                                NOW.

They Were Dancing

A Peoplehood *Real Time* short spoken word play in one to four parts for one to four actors

By Jaisey Bates

Jaisey Bates creates nontraditional collaborative work centering Global Majority perspectives with their theater company, The Peoplehood. They are a recipient of Marin Theatre Company's Emerging American Playwright Prize, an alumni of Playwrights Foundation, Cutting Ball Theater and Native Voices at the Autry festivals, and a finalist for the Princess Grace Award, O'Neill NPC, and American Blues Theater Blue Ink Award. www.the-peoplehood.com

[i.]
_____

THEY WERE DANCING
June 12, 2016
49 killed. 53 injured.
The Pulse, Orlando, FL

ALL: 'THE WORST SHOOTING IN U.S. HISTORY.'

ONE: Before Eddie Justice wrote

TWO: *"I love you mommy"*

ONE: they were dancing

THREE: A night

FOUR: A summer night

TWO: A night club

THREE: Community

FOUR: Sanctuary

ONE: The pulse

TWO: Music

THREE: Lights

FOUR: Laughter

ONE: Bodies in motion

ALL: BEFORE

ONE: Before staccato shots and shattered glass
Before the screams
Before bodies without motion
Before 49 souls stunned from their shells rise
Before those who escape and those 53 who survive with broken bodies
Leave their Before and begin long journeys toward Life After
Before loved ones shared memories of the victims who with

TWO: JUSTICE

ONE: lost their lives – before those lost lives exceed the ever-expanding

	borders of our current cartography of collateral loss to a point where the math does not compute – cannot compute
TWO:	Beyond this line there be
ALL:	…
TWO:	Beyond this line there be
ALL:	…
ONE:	Before we seek once again to compass and understand the
ALL:	IMPOSSIBLE
ONE:	Before a man enters Before he starts to shoot BEFORE ORLANDO They were dancing.
THREE:	Rewind.
FOUR:	Replay:
ONE:	A summer night. An Orlando club. They dance.

                A man enters – takes aim –
                people cry – people die –
                Justice hides – he texts his mother

THREE: *"In the club*

FOUR: *they shooting"*

ONE: beautiful, living dreaming loving beloved people who live through or do not survive these eternal suspended inconceivable moments as sheer terror unfolds in agonies, horrors … in one last reaching out
Thought

                Breath

                        heart
                        beat   …

        silenced because one person

TWO: One

THREE: More

FOUR: Person

ONE: made a choice to rob others of all of theirs.

[ii.]

THEY WERE DANCING
June 12, 2016
49 killed. 53 injured.
The Pulse, Orlando, FL

ALL: 'THE WORST SHOOTING IN U.S. HISTORY.'

TWO: This is the worst -- each time is the worst – each time innocents perish – each time families are forever changed, forever maimed – each time prayers and candles and tears and a search for meaning but an absence of meaning and a human cry for action but empty words and promises and no gun control – each time hate and hates and black holes devoid of empathy and understanding find new homes and feed and feed and ravenously feed on rage and swell and expand and consume and grow thick and fat in corners until they expand into the open … into the words and actions and inactions of those who would lead our communities … our country … until they reach up to the sky and stretch as far as the eye can see and we look to each other and speak softly so we don't frighten our children and we say

ALL: THERE'S A STORM COMING.

TWO: Each time is the worst.

[iii.]

THEY WERE DANCING
June 12, 2016
49 killed. 53 injured.
The Pulse, Orlando, FL

ALL: 'THE WORST SHOOTING IN U.S. HISTORY.'

THREE: This is the worst but how can we possibly calibrate 'the worst' – how as humans can we reduce to hollow rational numbers the constellating catastrophes of each victim's stories radiating chaos of devastation through countless lives – this is the worst – but all those children – all those bright beginnings – in that school and that school and that school – and those adults who lost their lives trying to save them – and Wounded Knee and Sand Creek … hundreds of victims including women and children … this is U.S. History too – this is the worst too – each time – each time is the worst and why please

ALL: WHY

THREE: are we Americans so

ALL: CONSTITUTION-

THREE: -ALLY unable to evolve the founders' document parameter'd story via effective actions with IRL traction rather than PAC and interest group financed legislators' #PrayFor pleas as they stand on the law – stand against change – build that wall against action with inaction – say *Isn't it a*

32

shame – send tears and prayers in carefully curated press conference media microbyte moments whilst away from the cameras and lights in a small room the words an endless loop – *They're not me or mine – we're safe – we're ok – we're fine*

[iv.]

THEY WERE DANCING
June 12, 2016
49 killed. 53 injured.
The Pulse, Orlando, FL

ALL: 'THE WORST SHOOTING IN U.S. HISTORY.'

FOUR: Until the next and the next and prayers and candles and tears and horror and grief and victims and loved ones and words and words and words
Like these.
Sound
Fury

Signifying

ALL: ...
...

FOUR: And yet love is love is love is Love Is LOVE

ALL: IS.

FOUR: And we here on this ground trying to love and breathe and dream and dance and dance and dance – trying to keep ourselves and each other alive – trying to survive, to thrive – WE

ALL: ARE

FOUR: so beautiful – each of us such beauty and this story we write – this story of us – it can be worthy of our beauty… this beauty we share … if we dare – LET US DARE

ALL: LET US DARE

FOUR: to dream and write together a world worthy of our children …

	our children's children – LET US DARE
ALL:	LET US DARE
FOUR:	to write an America where people beautiful living dreaming loving beloved people can dance … walk … love … LIVE
ALL:	LIVE
FOUR:	without
ONE:	One
TWO:	More
THREE:	Person
FOUR:	legally enabled to make
ONE:	One
TWO:	More
THREE:	Choice
FOUR	to rob

ALL: ONE. MORE. PERSON.

FOUR: of all of theirs – to rob ONE MORE PERSON of all of their as-yet unwritten years so we've got to wake up get to work – change the words – change the way our worlds are worded because there's a storm coming.

ONE: Because we can't hit Rewind. Rewrite.

TWO: Because they were dancing.

THREE: Because our children are watching.

FOUR: Because Love

ALL: IS

FOUR: and We

ALL: ARE.

Orlando, 2:02a.m.

by Migdalia Cruz

Migdalia Cruz, 2023 DGF Legacy and 2025 Re-Focus/Roundabout Playwright, is a Bronx-born writer, lyricist, translator, and librettist with over 60 works performed in 150 venues across 40 cities in 12 countries. Her awards include the NEA, McKnight, NYSCA, TCG/Pew, and she was named the 2013 Helen Merrill Distinguished Playwright. Cruz's mentor María Irene Fornés at INTAR and Latino Chicago Theater Company nurtured her voice. She co-chairs the DGF Playwriting Fellows, mentors the Latinx Playwrights' Circle, and was listed on The Kilroys Web 2023. Migdalia, an alumna of New Dramatists, is a member of The Tent, a theater for "vintage" playwrights. Her new anthology of plays "The Impossible Plays of Migdalia Cruz," debuted October 2024, published by Tripwire Harlot Press.

Contact: Peregrine Whittlesey
pwwagy@aol.com

Time: 2:02a.m., on June 12, 2016.

Place: Pulse Nightclub in Orlando, FL and the place your soul goes once released from there.

A play for a Puerto Rican man & a Nuyorican woman, LOLO & LOLA.

(LOLO, a Puerto Rican Man, wearing a white guayabera tied in front to make a muscle shirt and blue jean shorts, 22, rises from a pile of red feathers. HE talks to the feathers like they are bodies.)

LOLO: Right place, wrong time. It's always about time:

Wrong time, right outfit. Time is a pulse, a rhythmical throbbing of blood through the arteries, a heartbeat, an electrical current, a light, a wave, a burst, a blast...

(The sound of a round of automatic gunfire. The feathers ruffle.

LOLA, a Nuyorican woman, 21, stands up out of the pile of feathers, dressed in a coordinating colors to LOLO, white shorts, blue top.)

LOLA: Uhn uhn. Not yet.

(The sound suddenly stops. A neon dance light sparkles on.)

First, let's talk about the place: a place for freedom to be who you want to be, to be who you always knew you were.

LOLO: A place for political meetings, building community, making history in the gay-friendliest city in the nation.

LOLO & LOLA: *(In Unison)* This ain't just Mickey Mouse up in here—

LOLA: —but he's here too, with Minnie!

LOLO: And we have a lot of humidity.

LOLA: I like to sweat.

(The sound of a rifle loading.)

That's right. I said sweat! Because it's always dance time in this town.

(The sound of gunfire segues into the sound of dance music.

Something like the song "Battle Cry" by Angel Haze & Sia plays.)

39

LOLO: We were built for celebration. We ran from our homes—and for me that was Cabo Rojo—to Orlando because we needed someplace safe to be—away from our blood family who couldn't accept us —

LOLA: —and this was it.

LOLA & LOLO: *(In Unison)* Safe. Let's dance.

> *(THEY dance, the feathers rise and swirl around them & the music recedes.)*

LOLO: Guess someone got mad we were having fun.

LOLA: Guess someone got mad we had made a family.

LOLO: This family created from tempo, from the central point of energy—a rhythmic throbbing; pulsating, vibrating, beating, pounding, a thrumming of an echo reverberating—

LOLA: The ring, boom, rumble that tells me I'm free tonight. I'm me tonight. Hey, dance with me.

> *(Music segues into a different song "Free" by Ultra Nate, slowly growing in volume.)*

LOLO: And then...

LOLA: And then...my side pulsed with pain.

LOLO: My chest throbbed.

LOLA: My head vibrated from the sound of the gunfire.

LOLO: And I thought of all the stupid things I had to say in my life:

LOLA: "Shake my hand—it's not catching."

LOLO: "You don't catch AIDS from toilet seats."

LOLA: "You're not gay if you just think about waking up in the morning with your legs wrapped around someone your father won't approve of."

LOLO: Oh, that's real gay. But it's more than that. I know who I want to wake next to me in the morning. I know who I want to slow-dance with. I know who I want to plant a garden with.

LOLA: If you can't love me today, maybe you'll love me tomorrow.

LOLO: You don't have to understand me—just love me. That's the last thing I told my mom. I think she understands now.

(The music builds. Ultra Nate's "Free" segues into "Viva Puerto Rico Libre" by the Ghetto Brothers. LOLO & LOLA do a salsa step & turn.)

I imagined how this would all end. All this beauty!

(THEY strike a pose and laugh at themselves.)

LOLA: Not here though. Never here.

My journey to myself never ended like this.

LOLO: There was dope music and sweet laughter and tears of remembering.

LOLA & LOLO: *(In unison)*

What will they remember now?

(LOLO & LOLA walk to the patio door. All the neon in the club turns on for a moment as the feathers follow them out, like a trained feather boa. Then the lights go out.)

End of Play

The Gun Collector

By Nathan Alan Davis

Nathan Alan Davis's plays include *The Refuge Plays* (Roundabout Theatre in collaboration with NYTW), *Nat Turner in Jerusalem (NYTW)*, *The High Ground* (Arena Stage), *Eternal Life Part 1* (Wilma Theatre), *Origin Story* (Cincinnati Playhouse in the Park), *The Wind and the Breeze (Cygnet Theatre), and Dontrell Who Kissed the Sea (Skylight Theatre/NNPN Rolling World Premiere)*. In recognition of his body of work, Nathan has received a Windham-Campbell Prize (2021), a Steinberg Playwright Award (2020), and a Whiting Award in Drama (2018). Other honors include: Playwrights' Center Venturous Fellowship, Stavis Playwright Award, Steinberg/ATCA New Play Citation, Rita Goldberg Fellowship, and NYTW 2050 Fellowship. Nathan is an alumnus of the University of Illinois, Indiana University, and the Juilliard School. He is the Director of MFA Playwriting at Boston University.

Contact: Di Glazer, Creative Artists Agency 212-277-5287 diana.glazer@caa.com

A bare stage.

An Old Woman enters, pushing a grocery cart. The grocery cart is piled impossibly high with guns. Old guns. Modern guns. Futuristic guns. Pistols. Assault Rifles. Rocket launchers. Guns of every type and size imaginable.

The Old Woman rolls the cart to the center of the stage. She stops. She looks out at the audience.

OLD WOMAN

I went door to door.

How else?

…

…

(she looks at her cart)

…

It's not nearly enough, but I need to rest just a bit.

Part of getting old is that the heart still leads, but the body doesn't follow.

So that's why you might see someone like me, you know, sitting on a bench. Looking off into the distance.

I wish I had a bench to sit on now, but that's alright.

I can still look off into the distance.

(she looks off into the distance)

…

…

My heart wants to comb the earth like wind

And snatch up every godforsaken gun in the world,

Even the old ones,

Even the decorative ones.

The keepsakes,

The ancient muskets sitting in museums—

If we need mementos from our wars

Let's keep the bloodstained clothes instead—

Whisk away every last gun in the world: That's what my heart wants to do.

Even the water guns,

Even the very tiny plastic guns on little toy soldiers.

All of them.

That's what my heart wants.

…

(she turns around and laboriously walks to her cart)

You've heard, of course, about the swords and plowshares.

But these?

(she picks up a gun)

Can you make a plowshare out of this? I don't know. Maybe a computer.

(she puts the gun back)

(she begins to push the cart)

I just needed to catch my breath, time to hit the road again.

Well.

Hit.

Hit the road.

We are a violent people, aren't we?

Why not *touch* the road?

…

That wouldn't make sense to us. "Why are you *touching* the road?" We'd ask all sorts of questions.

(she begins to push the cart)

(she stops)

…

I wish I could tell you a beautiful story

About an angry man, clinging to his shotgun, who was changed when I looked into his eyes.

…

That's not quite how it's worked thus far.

I was somewhere. A forest. I asked a man for his rifle. He said "I'm a hunter". As if that was all he needed to say.

And I said, "Well if you're a hunter, why not use a spear? Or a bow and arrow.? Or you know, just run the mammoth off a cliff? That's what real hunters do. They chase their prey for miles and miles for hours and hours and hours. A whole day if they have to."

He looked at me like I was a child.

I said "You're not a hunter. You're a shooter."

He didn't seem to think there was any difference.

He told me to move on.

(she moves her cart)

(she stops)

How long do you think it will take me to disarm the world?

A thousand years?

Ten thousand?

A hundred thousand?

Do you believe it can be done?

My own son carries a gun.

I can't even get his.

We had dinner and I told him, "Honey,"

This was hard for me to say:

"Honey," I said,

"You just need to accept the fact that at any moment, someone might kill you. That's the reality of the world. That's the reality of a gun. It kills suddenly. That's what we've made. And until we unmake that reality, we have to live in it.

Unmake that reality. Start with yourself. Or you're part of the problem."

That's what I told him.

"Mom," he said,

"I love you, mom, but you're not being rational."

He's right, of course.

He's very, very right.

...

...

Once I get all the way around the world, I'll empty my cart. I'm sure I can find an active volcano somewhere to dump these in.

And then I'll go around again.

And on the second time around, maybe I'll do a little better.

And on the third time around maybe I'll do better than that. Maybe I'll be more patient. Or a better listener. Or more brave. Whatever is needed.

Maybe by the third time around, people will recognize me. I'll have earned a little trust.

And on the fourth, a little more.

And the fifth,

And the sixth,

Well you can see where I'm going, can't you?

However many revolutions it takes,

That's how many I'll make.

I'm a revolutionary!

Ha!

(sings)

I'm a revolutionary.

(she rings a bell on her grocery cart. she exits with it.)

Matted

A short response After Orlando

By Georgina Escobar

Georgina Escobar is a Mexican writer & maker of frontera futurity and musical femmetasias. She works with impossible narratives to excavate Latin American perspectives & create unique genre stories with heart. She is a MacDowell Fellow, Djerassi Artist, Fornés, & La Mama Umbria writer and recipient of the Kennedy Center's Darrell Ayers and the Outstanding Service to Women on the Border Award. Her work has been on the Kilroy's List, and at NAMT New York & NMTC at the O'Neill and produced internationally in México, UK, Italy, Denmark, and Sweden. Her work has been developed & produced at INTAR, New York Children's Theatre, Dixon Place, Clubbed Thumb, Hartford Stages, Lincoln Center, Bushwick Starr, Two Rivers, Milagro, Aurora Theatre, and People's Light.

Contact: Bonnie Davis, Bret Adams, Ltd, 448 West 44th Street, New York - NY 10036
bdavis@bretadamsltd.net

AT RISE

We are in a girl's bathroom at a night club.

Three stalls with closed doors.

In the distance, the pulsating sounds of a dance club at full force. We sit with that for a minute

Then:

BARTENDER (O.S.)

(*over mic*)

And now ladies and queens, here is a tune to remind us, that we all must go home at some point tonight. Last call everyone. Last call.

The song "At Last" by Etta James plays loudly overhead.

Then:

BANG. Could that be a gun, or is it fireworks? It's hard to— BANG BANG

PANIC.

Now visible from behind one of the stalls, two feet dangle. The feet and shoes are muddy, and bloody. They obviously belong to a little girl.

Then screams grow, Etta's voice sounds as if she were underwater, the sound of bullets ripping through the air in super slow speed: a requiem of drowned chaos

Until:

The door to the bathroom SLAMS open.

SASHA a latinx drag queen dressed as Selena enters, her gemmed bra is drenched in blood.

Panting, and desperate she moves to the first stall.

The lights flicker as she tries to pry it open.

Spotlight.

VOICE

(behind the stall)

Hey get outta here you pervert! You don't belong here! You don't belong here you monster!

SASHA

Please, I'm dying —

She removes her matted wig.

ANOTHER VOICE

(from same stall)

All of yous' should be. This is our bathroom. Beat it.

Sasha runs to the last stall and goes to open it.
The lights flicker and out come the sounds of:

CONGRESSMAN Y

(from behind closed stall, in Congressman voice)

It's in use! We are busy. We are very, very busy. There is work. To be done. Busy.

SASHA

He's after me. Please!

CONGRESSWOMAN X

(from behind closed stall)

I know! Write: " We believe the right of parents to determine the proper treatment or therapy, for their minor children."

CONGRESSMAN Y

How am I supposed to write this down if I don't have a pen?

CONGRESSMAN Y

Use the—here use this…blood. Use the blood here. Use it. Excuse me?

A hand from under the stall, like someone asking for toilet paper.

CONGRESSMAN Y

Can we use some of your blood to—we need to write policy. Politics. Polly-wanna-cracker…

A snicker from the middle stall.

Sasha knocks open the door to the middle stall.

In it, sits MADDIE ROSS. She is in full True Grit attire, and looks like she just rolled out of a movie set or a nightmare. She rolls a cigarette. A rifle leans beside her.

She looks up at Sasha just as she licks the paper.

SASHA

And who the hell are you?

MADDIE

What's it to you.

SASHA

There's a shooter and—

MADDIE

Shhh. He'll hear you.

SASHA

Am I dead?

MADDIE

You're dying. Maybe.

SASHA

Are you?

MADDIE

Smoke?

Gunshots. Sasha joins Maddie in the crammed stall.

He weeps. She rubs his bald head.

SASHA

I don't hear nothing no more.

MADDIE

Don't mean he's gone. Predators aint what they used to be, no sir. Used to be eye fer an eye down west. Now it's lead. Lead for rain. I like your head.

SASHA

(RE rifle)

That yours?

MADDIE

Sure is.

SASHA

You know how to work it?

CONGRESSMAN X

(on other stall)

He's trying to take our guns!

VOICE

(other stall, whispering)

Make sure a liberal gets in. It makes sales peak when people think they're takin' them away.

MADDIE

Who you afraid of more? The gun or their words?

SASHA

The echoes of hatred follow you even in death.

MADDIE

You aint dead.

SASHA

Yet.

MADDIE

"Yet"s all we got.

SASHA

I's so quiet. I don't know if I've ever felt this much stillness in my life.

MADDIE

It's silence.

Neither quiet nor still. Hate is heavy. Clings to you like summer, hangs on to your pipes like swallowin' salt water.

SASHA

This place's my home. It's my sanctuary...

VOICE 2

(from stall)

Shut it faggot, we're trying to hide.

SASHA

Why are they hiding? Why are they hiding in my home? This, is the time of beasts...

MADDIE

It's the time of cowards.

SASHA

And you plan to hunt them down? With that?

MADDIE

Nah. I'm saving my bullet. For revenge. Blood tastes sweeter the less it's spilt. You spill too much blood you spoil the hunt. You ruin the craft. You ruin the reason. You ruin the self. Killin' like that? Ain't about bein' nothin' but a coward. "Little trigger finger coward." That's what we'd call 'im. Back where I'm from.

SASHA

Who are you?

MADDIE

First woman you ever wanted to be.

SASHA

Only woman I've ever really wanted to be was...Maddie Ross...From the western.

MADDIE

The one and only.

SASHA

Brave Little Maddie Ross.

MADDIE

Aint' nothing but size that's little about me. But Now I'm your Brave Maddie Ross. So go on now. Be brave.

SASHA

How?

MADDIE

Stay livin'. Livin' is a hell of a task. Be brave and do that for me?

SASHA

Stay alive...

MADDIE

Yeah. Just that. You still gotta pulse, you go. It's how it goes.

SASHA

And revenge?

MADDIE

Don't you worry 'bout that. I got one bullet and it's worth more than all theirs together. It don't kill neither… Just you wait…But for now: Live on. Wake up. Wake up.

VOICES
Wake up. Wake up, Sasha. Hello. Miss? Hello? Please.

A White Out.

MADDIE (V.O.)

Go.

END OF PLAY.

Orlando monologue
By Lindsey Ferrentino

Lindsey Ferrentino is a playwright and screenwriter. Her plays include *Ugly Lies the Bone, Amy and the Orphans, The Flat Earth, The Year to Come, The Fear of 13* and the book for the musical *The Queen of Versailles*. She is developing several projects for Netflix.

For performance rights contact Ally Shuster at ally.shuster@caa.com

I stand in my grandparents' house...

They have always lived off the B-line, five minutes from the airport, in the backyard of SeaWorld.

The crack-crack of SeaWorld's fireworks hit the sky and knock at the tin rooftop of their Florida room.

I stand with my feet on their peach painted pavement and try to look at the red, white, and blue pops over the palm trees, being sent up a cooperation I loved as a child, but can no longer as an adult, after seeing a documentary that you HAD to see, but I knew would cast a spell on all those hot summer days I spent in line to get into the Shamu-show where the fireworks are currently being sent off from.

I try to look at the sky.

I stand in my grandparents' house underneath clouds set on fire with red, white, and blue.

I stand in my grandparent's retirement home.

That I used to joke was decorated in the colors of white, glass, and tile.

I thought they were rich.

Because they took us out for all meals--- to my favorite restaurant, on International Drive, which had buckets of free peanuts on the tables.

When I cracked the shells, I got to throw them on the floor like a glorious, gluttonous, tourist child-king.

My grandma, a frugal Jewish retiree, would open her purse and, dumping the peanuts into her bag, ask for a refill. My mom would be so embarrassed of my grandmother, hoarding these peanuts.

She'd say, *Jesus, I'll just buy you some. You know how much peanuts are? You can afford to buy peanuts.*

My grandmother would dump them anyway.

Not into a ziplock, just loose, hundreds of big salty peanuts into her vinyl white purse.

And we went to theme parks with my supposedly rich grandparents who didn't walk, but rolled through hand-capped lines on Disney's free motorized wheelchairs, more evidence of their apparent wealth, who took me out for meals at places where I could throw trash on the floor; where my drink came with a tiny pink umbrella.

I stand in my grandparents' house.

I try to look at the sky.

Through their Florida room.

That's what it's actually, architecturally called.

It buzzes with the ever-present low-lying suffocating heavy-hot air I've grown up in.

It buzzes from the heat of their old computer.

Which they only use for e-mail.

They literally log on to AOL.

I didn't even think this technology still existed, out in the world, that you had to "log on" and no one can call the house when you're "online' but apparently it does still exist because they have it.

The room is smelly with the mildewed futon used for guests; used for me when I stay at my grandparents house in their Florida room.

Next to this is my grandfather's "mail desk" where he actually sits down to pay his bills, devotes an entire afternoon to it. Licking envelopes, writing checks.

He doesn't know this can be done "online."

He thinks "online" is a place to be e-mailed dirty jokes.

He likes to save these dirty jokes, so he asks me to print them out for him on paper.

So he can save them in actual files, in a cabinet, in his bill-paying desk, so he won't lose them.

I grew up one hour outside of where they live in Orlando.

A straight shot on the B-line, we'd say.

Forty-five minutes towards the beach.

That's where I live and

my grandparents live in Orlando.

32821.

The same zip-code as Nickelodeon studios.

Where as a kid, I sent countless postcards into a raffle, hoping they'd pick me to be on television covered in slime.

My supposedly rich grandparents live in the shadow of a captive orca whale.

And in Orlando, the sky turns red white and blue from Seaworld's finale.

And when people ask me where I'm from, I say

One hour outside of Orlando.

When I book my ticket home to see my family, I fly into Orlando International Airport.

I don't even look up the airport code because I know it by heart.

MCO.

And when I moved to Florida in fifth grade from New York, my classmates promised we'd be friends forever.

They would write everyday.

They only wrote once and it was a picture of Mickey Mouse and me, lying on the beach.

There's palm trees and ferris wheels and whales jumping into the sky in front of fireworks lighting up red, white, and blue.

Say hello to Mickey for me!

You get to live where we take our vacations.

I can't believe you're going to live in paradise!

And in Orlando I turn twelve.

And celebrate my birthday party in a science museum in an upside down building, next to Ripley's Believe it or Not.

And in Orlando, where the better malls are, I shop for back-to-school clothes.

In Orlando, I go to grad night at Magic Kingdom, still seventeen, covered in foam the DJ shoots out, as we wait to see Mandy Moore, holding glow sticks.

And in Orlando, I visit on college breaks.

And my grandparents mail me newspaper clippings that remind them of me.

Hand-written from the bill paying desk, marked with 32821.

And only my grandparents, my family, and me and the Disney commercials say the city name *Orlando*.

It isn't a place you particularly need to talk about much.

And in Orlando, I curl my grandmother's hair when she is released from the hospital.

In Orlando, I help her go through her things.

Down-sizing she says, even though no one is moving.

We throw away birthday cards she bought on sale, but never sent and now won't have time to.

We find uneaten peanuts at the bottom of most of her bags.

In the Florida room, they move my grandmother to a hospice bed.

And my grandmother tells me they chose to move to Orlando when they retired to get some rest.

And in Orlando, the city of retirees, another old person dies another death.

And then my grandfather dies too, suddenly, drops dead in his kitchen.

His best friend Al tells us not to have a funeral, cause no one'll come, cause most of my grandparent's friends are dead too.

He says the next funeral he's going to is his own.

He says he moved to Orlando for the easy life style.

The predictable weather.

For my grandparents.

And now their house is empty.

That *still* sort of empty where once there were people, but now there's furniture.

And an old computer nobody wants.

And purses with peanut shells.

And a bill-paying desk stuffed with dirty jokes.

Mattresses with sheets still on them and toothbrushes, lipstick, dirty slippers, and a toaster oven-- what's left after death.

And my mom has to clear it out, item by item. To Goodwill. To the trash. To her siblings. To herself.

She jokes that next time her parents die, she'll know how to plan better.

I want to stand in their Florida room, but the house was sold and now it belongs to someone else.

And we don't speak of this city anymore in my family.

The place I'd go and talk about is now only ever heard on Disney commercials.

Until one day, my mom asks if I've seen the news.

I remember thinking that's a very general "mom" question to ask.

When. What news? About what.

Orlando, she says.

In a place right off of International Drive.

What?

By that restaurant- you know, the one with the peanuts.

What?

Behind the good mall.

Right there, she says.
It's sort of near the up-side down building where you had your birthday party one year, you remember that place?

How well do you remember Orlando,

she asks me---

Trying to explain where it happened.

But all I can see are my two feet,
Standing barefoot on a slab of peach pavement in my grandparent's Florida room,
their American dream,
while I sweat

and smell mildew

and the staleness of death

and choke in the heat

feeling the ground shift beneath me

shaking.

I try to look at the sky for fireworks

And everything around me is already rumbling.

Pistols (an action in six parts)

By Andy Field

Andy Field is an artist and writer based in London, England. He creates projects that invite people to consider their relationship to the places they live and the people they live with. Over the last decade this has manifested itself across a range of forms and disciplines, including street games, event scores, installations, studio theatre shows and one-to-one performances. A key strand of Andy's practice involves making work in collaboration with young people with the aim of enabling them to play a meaningful part in the civic discourse of the cities and towns in which they live. www.andytfield.co.uk

Note

When invited to write something in response to the events at Pulse Nightclub in Orlando I had no words. Any attempt at representation through fiction felt inadequate.

Instead I looked as I often have toward the work of American conceptual artist and avant-garde composer George Brecht, as a way of inviting the audience and the performers to at least experience something together. The shape and tone of this short event score is indebted to him. This work has no greater meaning or symbolism. It is offered only as an opportunity for any particular audience and any performer to figure something out together in that ambiguous space between them.

As such any new performance is an invitation to interpret these simple instructions in any way that feels appropriate for that context, be that joyful, solemn, raucous or restrained.

1

Performer fires water pistol at the audience

2

Audience fires waters pistols at the performer

3

Performer throws flowers at the audience

4

Audience throws flowers at the performer

5

Performer takes photographs of the audience

6

Audience take photographs of the performer

The Healing Power of Bright Colors

By Ryan Gielen

Ryan Gielen is a writer/director in Los Angeles. Works include short plays produced by Fundamental Theater Project (NYC), STICKY (NYC), Missing Bolts (NYC), No Passport (NYC), Mass Rhetoric (Los Angeles), and the documentary *My Beautiful Stutter*, from executive producer Paul Rudd and Discovery Channel.

OPEN ON: EMMA.

Tank top, shorts, beach towel under one arm, a hard cover book in her other hand. She's around 30, slight, and her voice is soft and child-like.

EMMA: They say the only thing stopping a bad guy with a gun is a good guy with a gun. It makes sense, if you think about it. After all, once every country had missiles, there was no more war.

Beat.

I'd like to follow this to its logical conclusion. I'd like to insist that everyone be armed. Everywhere. At all times. Including on airplanes. I think it would be fun to see how the arm rest situation resolves itself when both the tiny grandma in twentyseven-B and the giant bodybuilder in twenty-seven-C are packing heat.

Beat.

I once had to catch a five a.m. flight across the country after a wedding the night before. I was deeply, profoundly hungover and the two people behind me really hit it off. They spent the entire three and a half hours loudly comparing their Gluten intolerances. I would have liked to have been armed on that flight.

She mimics turning around in her seat, half-assedly pointing a gun in their faces.

"Shut up, or I will jam so much bread down your throat that you will become Gluten."

Beat.

Although, perhaps that's why it's best that no one is armed on flights. Not everyone is as stable as I am. Am I allowed to say that? That massacres of innocent civilians are committed by the mentally ill? I have a hard time keeping up with which singular narrative I'm allowed to discuss after any given massacre. One little thought exercise: is it possible to single-handedly massacre innocent civilians if you're not mentally ill?

Beat.

He was a lone wolf who played too many video games. He was an Islamist sympathizer who daydreamed of joining ISIS. He was a jilted employee who kept to himself mostly. He was a white supremacist who believed anarchy would return the nation to its Aryan roots. He was a closet case whose religion drove him to violent self-hatred.

Beat.

He, he, he. He is, he was, he believed, he wanted, he preached, he hated. He, he, he.

Beat.

He. He. He.

Beat.

Seems like these mass killings have a running theme. Am I allowed to talk about that? The cult of masculinity? I don't want to chop anyone's balls off. But I would like to acknowledge the difference between those of us who end up in Grey Gardens and those who end up in, say, Pulse Nightclub last night.

Beat.

I'm on vacation here in sunny Orlando, commonly referred to by locals and in travel brochures as "The Happiest City on Earth." A vacation with myself! Just me. And a good book. And some wine.

And a wonderful little contraption that my friend from California sent me on my birthday. It's called a vape, and it's the single best invention of this millennium. I'm going to get high as a kite, read my book, and bake in the sun for the next eight hours.

She turns to leave, stops.

They say the only thing stopping a bad guy with a gun is a good guy with a gun. That's not a public health philosophy, that's a pitch to a 1940's studio boss.

> *Beat.*

We are such children.

> *She reads from the cover*
> *of her book.*

"The Healing Power of Bright Colors." Elizabeth Gilbert's new one. Jesus. We are all such children.

> *She pulls deeply on the vape as she exits.*

Baby Sister: A Monologue Play

By Jacqueline Goldfinger

Jacqueline Goldfinger is an award-winning playwright, dramaturg, and librettist. Her work has been produced around the world, including performances at The John F. Kennedy Center for the Performing Arts (USA), Sydney Opera House (Australia), Contemporary American Theatre Festival (USA), École nationale de théâtre (Canada), BBC Radio 3 (UK), Disquiet (Portugal), Chiesa di Ognissanti (Italy), and Court Theatre (New Zealand). She's the author of "Playwriting with Purpose: A Guide and Workbook for Playwrights" (Routledge). She's taught playwriting and dramaturgy at University of Pennsylvania, UC Davis, and others. Jacquelinegoldfinger.com

(A young woman from rural Florida, just outside Orlando:)

(a moment of trying to tell a memory that's blurred from the overwhelming of it)

Naw, they said.

Naw, just come on down, don't feel the,

Or worry about it. Nothin' to… whatever.

It's not his, blood, or, viscera, or, whatnot.

It's just,

Come on down, please.

Come for him.

(avoidance of painful memory)

They musta' learned that word, that "viscera," learned it off the television.

It sounds like a made up word for the T.V.

Like it's foreign. Or a lie.

It sounds like…, don't know.

But, my brother,

My brother itn't no viscera. He's not, pieces, or butchered hog.

He's a man.

I just seen him the other day.

Anyways.

(sometimes it's more painful to think of him alive than dead)

(a decision to tell the story)

Momma heard tell from the police, on the other end of the line.

They give her a call and say "it's your son" and she say, "sure as shit it ain't," and hung up on 'em.

And she calls me up, say, "you not believe what they say."

And I say,

"Yes ma'am, no ma'am, a crazy thing, ma'am."

She goes on and I hear the name of the station they called up from.

Orlando.

He'd been in Orlando for the night.

All out the interstate in that big city mess.

So I call the 911 and say "I need to talk to 'em. I need my brother."
Then I just sit there on hold.

Run my fingers round and round the broken hem of my nightdress; swayin' and askin' Jesus for one last miracle.

Anyways.

I's the one that picks him,

Picks up the body.

I have to sign for him. Like I'd ordered him from Amazon or some….

Bullshit, what it was!

Signin' for him like a, a, a, a, I don' know.

But it just

Pissed

Me

Off.

Handlin' him like he's a carcass. Like he's somethin' they own. Like, a pay out at the track.

I got a receipt for my brother.

(calms self down)

I mean, they aren't...,

They are all real nice.

They are the nicest folks.

They say real nice things about him, his friends.

They want to meet Momma.

But,

She weren't never comin'. Not now.

Not now that she knows.

Hearin' that, the not comin',

That just makes them quiet.

His friends.

The police.

The victims helper lady.

They aren't like what folks say in Church, or over at the 7-11, or

At all the other lit up places I go.

They are nice.

Brother was nice. And looked nice.

They, the police, wrapped him up when they gave him back.

'Cause all the damage.

I couldn't seen him no more. They didn't recommend it.

But he's always a real pretty boy.

So pretty I used to put his school picture over top of mine on the fridge. I'd magnet his picture directly over my face because he looked so fine and I looked like a gator fucked a muppet. Never my best years. But he always shined in his school picture.

And he's nice actin', too, and funny to boot.

Not snort-Co-Cola-through-your-nose funny but like, small things observed, funny.

Like when we's little, he'd say to me,

"Look, look at that spider web!

With that dew on it.

Don't it look like a fairy wing? Come right down here to earth?

We must be something special if we're allowed to see that.

You and me, me and you, peanut butter and jelly.

Special for us. We are so blessed."

He always could see things no one else could.

Like me.

And I could see him.

And I didn't never tell nobody what he really was.

It was like he had a super power and I was helping him keep it a secret.

Anyways.

After I left them, I went right back home,

But we couldn't bury him in our church yard.

We couldn't because,

I mean, we could but,

The Church yard asked me not to bring him.

On account of the family and the family plot.

Momma had already called over and said he wouldn't be welcome in it.

The Church yard man thought it'd be best, tasteful, respectful, if I,

Moved him on along.

To somewhere else.

It'd be more Christian of me.

And I guess, I guess I shoulda' said "okay" and hung up then. But…

I told him I's a Christian and so's my brother.

We all got things, got private things with the Lord,

But that don't mean we can't be buried together. We're family.

We are family!
Wearefamilywearefamilywearefamilywearefamilywe arefamilywearefamilywe

Arefamilywearefamilywearefamilywearefamilyweare familywearefamilywearefamilywearefamilyweare-

And Mr. Church Yard is all quiet. For a long time.

And then he says I should turn my sights another way.

He said he wouldn't open the cemetery gates for us.

Then the grave digger hangs up on me.

And I put my end down too.

I don't know what grasped me to say that.

I don't know how I,

I don't talk like that.

I just,

You know,

"Yes, ma'am."

"No, ma'am."

"Sorry, sir. So so sorry."

But in that moment,

It's like,

Brother came right out my lips.

His voice, right out my mouth.

In that moment, he made me unafraid.

To say what need to be said.

He made me strong.

He made me sure.

So I did turn around.

I drove the other way.

I found him a beautiful place, under the oaks and the Spanish moss, in the welcome shade, to rest.

A place like where we saw that spider web.

And I buried him.

And I quit my crappy job and got another crappy job

In a town where I can be close to him.

With his strength in my back pocket and his love on my lips.

We're gonna start again.

And this time, we're not afraid of anybody.

(end of monologue)

He Comes Up Behind Me

By. Garret Jon Groenveld

Garret Jon Groenveld is a poet and playwright in San Francisco (MFA in Poetry/MA in Playwriting from SFSU). He also studied with Edward Albee at the University of Houston. A founding writer of PlayGround, his plays include DISBELIEF, SACRIFICE, MISSIVES, THE SERVING CLASS, THE HUMMINGBIRDS and THE EMPTY NESTERS.

>Contact: 300 Buchanan St., #103
>San Francisco, CA 94102
>Email: thegroenster@gmail.com

ABEL and JIM getting ready to go out. JIM is in his pants and a tank top ironing a shirt

ABEL: When will you be done?

JIM: I'm ironing my shirt.

ABEL: Why?

JIM: So it looks nice.

ABEL: Oh my god –stop being <u>that</u> queen and hurry up! I want to dance.

JIM: I want to look nice.

ABEL: Oh. (*teasing*) For your … boyfriend?

JIM: You don't think he's cute?

ABEL: We have very different tastes. Me? I like them taller – but for you, yes. He's very cute.

JIM: I know right? Those eyes! With the lashes and the – oh! So handsome.

ABEL: Very your type. You like the eyes. With you – it's all about the eyes. What's his name again?

JIM: Rafael. (*A pause.*) I think it's Rafael. It was loud. It could just be Rafa.

ABEL: You don't know his name?

JIM: It was loud. There. I'm done.

He's finished ironing his shirt – he starts to put it on.

ABEL: I didn't know you were into Hispanic guys.

JIM: I'm into all kinds of guys.

ABEL: (*Aside and coughing:*) Slut! (*full voice:*) Do you think he even likes white guys?

JIM: I don't know. I hadn't thought much about it.

ABEL: Maybe he doesn't like white guys.

JIM: I don't know. I think he likes me. He liked my jeans.

ABEL: He likes your ass in those jeans.

JIM: It <u>is</u> pretty good right?

ABEL: He couldn't keep his hands off of you.

JIM: He liked the way I danced. I liked the way he danced.

ABEL: You liked how close you two danced together. How do you even know he's going to be there?

JIM: I don't know – and it is Latino night. And he did ask me if I was going to be there next time.

ABEL: You speak Spanish?

JIM: He spoke English! Why are you giving me such a hard time? I like him.

ABEL: Then I like him too – I just want to go. Are you ready? You look great.

JIM: Really?

ABEL: He's going to love you madly and want to marry you tomorrow.

ABEL: You think so?

JIM: Sure – absolutely, just get his digits this time? Now - can we get out of here? I want to dance!

JIM: Yes – Let's go -

ABEL: Let's dance –

– *A shift – ABEL and JIM are now at the dance club and do a slow motion salsa move. Music.*

JIM: And I don't see Rafael there, at least not when we get there. But I look good. I feel good. I'm happy to just hang out with my best friend, so we just dance a while. After a while, he finds someone else to dance with, so I dance alone a bit. (*ABEL disappears and JIM imagines the following – in a salsa motion.*) And then Rafael finally gets there. I didn't see him at first, he comes up behind me on the dance floor – and he gives me a big hug. And it feels so good. He puts his hand on my hip and his whole arm around my chest. And I take his hand and lace my fingers into his. (*He feels this.*) And we dance like that for such a long time. I don't want it to stop. (*He stops dancing.*) And then we aren't dancing anymore. (*The music stops.*) And I hear a noise, a shot? (*He turns.*) So I turn around, and there is something going on over there, but I all I can look at is Rafael, standing right before me, and those lashes and his eyes. Those beautiful eyes.

Slow fade to black –

End.

We Are Molecules

by C. Julian Jiménez

C. Julian Jiménez - Queer, Puerto Rican/Dominican writer. MFA/The Actors Studio Drama School, Awards: New Dramatist Resident, 2019 Rita Goldberg Fellow, 2018 LaGuardia LGBTQ History Grant, & 2009 Public Theater's EWG fellow. Plays: *Bruise & Thorn, Julio Ain't Goin' Down Like That, Animals Commit Suicide, Locusts Have No King,* and *Alligator Mouth, Tadpole Ass.* Professor/Queensborough Community College.

CHARACTERS

ANGEL - A beautiful twenty-something Boricua man

LEFT BRAIN - A pessimist

RIGHT BRAIN - An optimist

> Lights up on ANGEL taunted by his LEFT and RIGHT brain.
>
> He dances to Bachata at the club.

LEFT BRAIN
    We are molecules.

RIGHT BRAIN
    We are love.

LEFT BRAIN
    Molecules.

RIGHT BRAIN
   Love.

LEFT BRAIN
   MOLECULES!

RIGHT BRAIN
   LOVE!

ANGEL
   Arms up in the air with slats of skin peeking through denim and cotton. Lights flashing, blinding through tightly shut eyelids. Boys to the left of me spraying beads of sweat. Their bodies gyrate against boys they just met. The bass is pumping, and I glide across the dance floor as if the ground beneath me was a slate of ice and I the Olympic champion, Oksana Baiul. But this is no frigid ice-skating rink, this is a sauna of erotic possibilities. A place where striking up a conversation with that statue of David doesn't need courage, because here rejection ain't scary... it just sucks.

LEFT BRAIN
   We should continue to be suspect.

RIGHT BRAIN
   We should let down our guard. We are home.

LEFT BRAIN
   Suspect.

RIGHT BRAIN
  Home.

LEFT BRAIN
  SUSPECT!

RIGHT BRAIN
  HOME!

ANGEL
  I see a man in the dancing rink... all shirtless with specks of glitter in his chest hair. He's just hugged a tragic queen with a lifted-up lace-front. He dances Bachata like a Eurotrash meth-head and somehow my heart pounds out my chest as if it is bait on a fishing line trying to reel him in. It does. The whole room goes into soft focus like we are Tony and Maria at the dance. I breathe in his testosterone sweat and Burberry ether and I am sent into a tailspin of longing and arousal.

LEFT BRAIN
  Smell is the processes of encoding, analyzing, and decoding information.

RIGHT BRAIN
  Smell is the heart's keepsake.

LEFT BRAIN
  Processes.

RIGHT BRAIN
Keepsake.

LEFT BRAIN
PROCESSES!

RIGHT BRAIN
KEEPSAKE!

ANGEL
Don't trip, Left and Right brain. There is no need to argue, this man across from me satisfies logic and imagination. Look at him. I mosey on over to this gorgeous specimen and place my hand on his hip. The music and the dance floor give me power to pursue what I can only look at as I walk down Orange Avenue.

LEFT BRAIN
This is unsafe.

RIGHT BRAIN
We are protected by these walls.

LEFT BRAIN
Unsafe.

RIGHT BRAIN
Protected.

LEFT BRAIN
UNSAFE!

RIGHT BRAIN
    PROTECTED!

ANGEL
    He places his hand on my hip. Our pelvises touch. We are forehead to forehead. A stream of sweat rolls down his head and mixes with mine. His moves are still Eurotrashesque, so I pull out my Zumba instructing skills and teach him proper Bachata rhythm. He falls perfectly in line. We dance. I am his teacher, and he is happily my student.

LEFT BRAIN
    Actually, this feels kind of okay.

RIGHT BRAIN
    Right? So. Okay.

ANGEL
    We dance. It's perfect. It's possibility in an 8 count.

LEFT BRAIN
    You may be on to something here, Right Brain.

RIGHT BRAIN
    Possibilities.

ANGEL
    We dance.

LEFT BRAIN
　　We dance.

RIGHT BRAIN
　　We dance.

ANGEL
　　We dance and....

LEFT BRAIN
　　And it feels so right.

RIGHT BRAIN
　　Totally. Right? We are love!

ANGEL
　　I feel...

LEFT BRAIN
　　Yes?

RIGHT BRAIN
　　Yes?

ANGEL
　　Alive!

> The music stops abruptly with a big pulsing bass sound that echoes through the end of the play.

                                        RIGHT BRAIN
                                        falls hard and
                                        quick. RIGHT
                                        BRAIN is gone.

                                        ANGEL stops
                                        dancing.

               (beat)

                                        LEFT BRAIN
                                        slowly falls to the
                                        ground.

LEFT BRAIN
    We are molecules.

                                        ANGEL stares out
                                        to the audience...

                                        Lights Down.

                                        END OF PLAY

Ally

by Alexander Kveton

Alexander Kveton's recent plays include *Masters, Allies, Feesh: A Memory Play,* and *Dean of Students.* His short film *The Short Goodbye* was presented at the New York Shorts International Film Festival and the Middlebury New Filmmakers Festival in 2019. His essay "Laughter and Its Uses" was published in the journal Contemporary Theatre Review. (alexanderkveton.com)

Characters:

MARK   male, white, mid-twenties, grad student

CHRIS   male, white, mid-twenties, grad student

Setting:

An apartment in a major city

Time:

June 16th, 2016

An apartment. Sound of an AC whirling. MARK at a computer. CHRIS close by on his phone. Both on social media.

MARK: I think some of the most dreaded words in the English language today are "I don't normally do this, but."

CHRIS: Yup.

MARK: Honestly, since when has Brad given a shit about anything?

CHRIS: Let me see.

(CHRIS searches on his phone.)

MARK: It's like, "way to go buddy, you're doing great."

CHRIS: I mean, better late than never.

MARK: But *that*?

CHRIS: True.

MARK: And yet people are on my shit for not saying anything.

CHRIS: Nobody called you out personally —

MARK: Still. I mean, you know. If you're my friend, you know I love you.

CHRIS: I know.

MARK: You should know that.

CHRIS: I know.

MARK : So then like, if I say something now, am I just being disingenuous? Am I being like Brad? How the hell can I say anything *now*?

> (MARK's phone vibrates. He silences it. The phone stays glowing for a couple beats as...)

CHRIS: If it would make you feel better —

MARK: If I'm going to tell someone I care about them, I'm going to send an email. I don't need everyone to see that I'm, *whatever*.

CHRIS: I mean, when you heard, did you think of Daveed and Ashley and —

MARK: Of course I did.

CHRIS: If you didn't that's —

MARK: Dude, of course I did, why wouldn't I've? But like, I didn't think anyone wanted to be reminded of it.

(MARK's phone vibrates and lights up again. He silences it.)

CHRIS: It's tough, no doubt about it. I texted Fran that day to see how she was doing and she said it really meant —

MARK: You texted Fran?

CHRIS: Yeah.

MARK: How'd you know to do that?

CHRIS: What do you mean? I just thought to do it.

MARK: Why didn't you tell me?

CHRIS: I didn't think to.

MARK: I just don't want to say something and seem like I don't mean it.

CHRIS: Okay.

MARK: (referring to the screen) What do you think? I don't sound like Brad, do I?

(MARK's phone vibrates and lights up for a third time. He silences it.)

CHRIS: Dude, I got to go the bathroom, I'll read it when — Jesus, who keeps calling you?

MARK: It's uh, it's Daveed.

CHRIS: Oh. What's he want?

MARK: I don't know, nothing important.

CHRIS: Shouldn't you —

MARK: Dude, I just need to finish this, if I don't I'll never —

CHRIS: I mean, he may be asking for —

MARK: No, it'll be fine. I'll call him after. He can wait.

CHRIS: Okay… Be right back then.

>*(Chris exits as Mark stares at his screen. He looks down at his phone, silent but still lit. He stares hard at his screen as the lights begin to fade. The phone stops glowing. He relaxes for a moment. The phone vibrates one more time signaling a voicemail. He looks at it. After a moment, the lights go to black.)*

everybody gets a stick

by Deborah Zoe Laufer

Deborah Zoe Laufer's plays have been produced at Steppenwolf, Cincinnati Playhouse in the Park, The Humana Festival, Everyman, Primary Stages, EST and hundreds of other theaters around the world. She is a graduate of Juilliard, an alumna of BMI, and a Dramatists Guild council member. DEBORAHZOELAUFER.com

Contact:

Deb Laufer
DZLaufer@Optimum.net
DeborahZoeLaufer.com
© 6/16

(Mrs. Smith and Ms. Jonas are in Principal Right's office.)

PRINCIPAL RIGHT:
Ms. Jonas. This is Mikey Smith's mother. She's very upset.

MRS. SMITH:
I'm very upset!

PRINCIPAL RIGHT:
She says you've taken away Mikey's stick and given him lunch detention. Is that right?

MRS. SMITH:
I gave Mikey that stick!

MS. JONAS:
Well, he's been hitting the other children.

PRINCIPAL RIGHT:
Did you ask him not to?

MS. JONAS:
Of course.

PRINCIPAL RIGHT:
Did you make it very clear that he can have the stick but only use it for self defense?

MS. JONAS:
No. I told him not to hit anybody. And I took away the stick.

MRS. SMITH:
He has a right to have the stick I gave him. And to play outside with the other kindergarteners!

MS. JONAS:
Well, how about this. I'd like to get him some counseling. And then, if we determine he's ready to play outside with the other children, he can. Without the stick.

MRS. SMITH:
Where does it say that in school policy?? Where does it say you can take away my child's stick? And his freedom??

MS. JONAS:
Well…

PRINCIPAL RIGHT:
She's absolutely right. So what we've done, we've ordered three hundred sticks so that all the children will have them.

MS. JONAS:
What?

MRS. SMITH:
What?

PRINCIPAL RIGHT:
And as soon as Mikey hits one of the children, all the other children can take a swing at him.

MRS. SMITH:
Oh. Well…

MS. JONAS:
That seems really dangerous. And his stick has a nail in it. It's not just an ordinary stick.

MRS. SMITH:
It's true. It's a high power stick.

PRINCIPAL RIGHT:
Yes, all the children's sticks will have nails in them.

MRS. SMITH:
Oh… umm… I don't know…

MS. JONAS:
That's terrible. Everyone will get badly hurt.

PRINCIPAL RIGHT:
But, they're good children, right? All the others? Are good?

MS. JONAS:
Of course. But that's not really /the point…

PRINCIPAL RIGHT:
Then it'll be fine. Good children with sticks will do the right thing.

MS. JONAS:
It'll be a bloodbath. Even *I* won't want to go out into the schoolyard.

PRINCIPAL RIGHT:
Well, we'll give you a nail stick too. All the faculty and students will have a nail stick. And of course, the cafeteria staff will have their knives.

MRS SMITH:
Oh dear. I'm not /sure that…

MS. JONAS:

Couldn't we just take away Mikey's stick?

MRS. SMITH:

No! You can't! You can't take away Mikey's stick!

PRINCIPAL RIGHT:

All right then! We're all on the same page!

MS. JONAS:

Will *you* be in the schoolyard with a stick?

PRINCIPAL RIGHT:

Oh no. I don't enforce the rules – I just make them. I'll be right here. In my office. With the door closed. And the blinds drawn. Enjoy your lunch!

And Then the Music...

by E.M. Lewis

(A Chorus for Six Voices and Six Drummers, After Orlando)

-written for After Orlando Theater Action 2016-

E. M. Lewis is an award-winning playwright and opera librettist, recipient of the Steinberg Award and Primus Prize from the American Theater Critics Association. Her work has been produced around the world, and published by Samuel French. She is the Mellon Foundation Playwright-in-Residence at Artists Repertory Theater. Member: Dramatists Guild.

emlewis.playwright@me.com

www.emlewisplaywright.com

Six drummers play a simple latin beat on drums or buckets. The beat starts slowly, but escalates over the course of the piece, changing in tone as indicated.

Six players stand on the empty stage, ready to dance. Happy to dance. Dancing!

1	(*loud, from the booth, setting the scene*) Amigos! Hermanos! Carinos! You ready to dance? Are you ready to--
2/3	Yeah!
1	--dance? Are you--
4/5	Turn it up!
1	--ready to dance?!
6	Hit me, baby!
5	And then the music--
3	--gets louder!!

The beat of the drums gets louder.

Everybody dances, alone.

And then...

2   Hey, guapa! Como estas?

3   Dance with me!

4   Where you from?

5   Venezuela. Where you from?

4   Puerto Rico.

5   Your mami know you dance like this?

4   She's right over there!

5   Oh, man! Look at her go!

6   Turn it up!

1   Baila! Baila! Baila!

5   You dance good.

4   You dance good.

3   You dance good.

2   You dance good.

1   And then the music--

6   --gets mas sexy...

The music and the dancing become sexier.
More intimate.

2   Why do you come here?

3   Only place I can be myself. You know?

2   Yeah.

3   Why do you come here?

2   Meet Prince Charming, muy guapo, somebody, somebody, somebody like you.

4   Why do you come here?

5   I don't know.

4   You don't know?

5   I like the music.

4   I like the music, too.

5   I like to dance.

4   I like to dance, too.

5   Nobody calls me faggot here.

4   Except affectionately.

5   Except affectionately. I'm not invisible here.

4   Nobody likes to be invisible.

5   I don't want to be invisible.

4   I see you.

1   Why do you come here?

6   Enrique Iglesias is my jam, man. He makes me so happy. Why do you come here?

1   I like making people happy.

4   And then the music gets--

2   --mas feliz!

6   Play some Enrique Iglesias!

4   Elvis Crispo!

3   Don Omar!

5   Shakira!

2   Whenever, Whatever...

4   Un Poco de Amor...

3   Hips Don't Lie!

1   You want it, you got it.

6   Everybody needs a place to dance.

2   Everybody needs a place to let their hair down.

3   Everybody needs a place to be themselves.

4   Everybody needs a place that's safe.

5   Everybody needs a place that's safe.

1   Everybody needs a place that's--

A shot rings out. (Use the drums, all hands smashing down.)

Actor 1 falls to the floor.

One drummer stops playing.

5   What was that?

2   Did you hear something?

3   Oh, my God.

6   Look out!

4   What's happening?

A shot rings out.

Actor 4 falls to the floor.

Another drummer stops playing.

5   No!

2   Hide!

3   Where? Oh, Jesus.

5   I just met you!

2   We can hide in the bathroom.

3   Come on!

5   I like you.

2   Hurry!

3   He's coming...

5   I liked you.

A shot rings out.

Actor 2 falls to the floor.

Another drummer stops playing.

3   Oh!

6   There's blood on the floor. So much blood on the--

A shot rings out.

Actor 6 falls to the floor.

Another drummer stops playing.

5	All he wanted to do was--
3	All he wanted to do was--
5	All he wanted to do was--
3	All he wanted to do was--
5/3	--dance.

A shot rings out.

Actor 5 falls to the floor.

Another drummer stops playing.

3   And then the music--

A shot rings out.

Actor 3 falls to the floor.

Silence.

Our Friends

by Joan Lipkin

Joan Lipkin, a recipient of both Visionary and Arts Innovator of the Year Awards among others, is a playwright, director, educator, producer and activist whose work is widely produced, anthologized and published including in "Best American Short Plays", "Every 28 Hours" "Lighting the Way: An Anthology of Short Plays About the Climate Crisis", "Amazon All Stars" and "Scenes from a Diverse World."
joan.lipkin@gmail.com

CHARACTERS

Alison – A white female, early 30's to mid 40's. She is the tougher one, at least on the outside. Usually funny and charming, she is undone by the Pulse massacre and vacillates between grief and rage. It is bringing up many things.

Samantha – A female of color, early 30's to mid 40's. She is softer, more conciliatory. She is upset about Pulse, too, but wants to move on and restore normalcy and that means routine.

These two women love each other and have very different coping mechanisms and responses to life and sometimes, that has been part of the attraction. But will this tragedy bring them closer together or break them apart?

In the interests of expansive possibilities for performance, these roles can also be played by college students. The racial or ethnic casting is up to the director or creative team.

SETTING

The apartment of Alison and Samantha, somewhere in a smaller or mid-sized city in the US, perhaps the midwest.

Time: A week after the massacre in Orlando.

(*At rise, Alison is sitting in front of the television watching repeat footage of the Pulse massacre. She has been wearing the same clothes for days. There are empty beer bottles around her. Samantha is dressed to go out and anxious to get going.*)

SAMANTHA. What do you mean, you can't go?

ALISON. Oh, so I should just eat dinner and make some fucking small talk? About what, Pokémon? Or listen to Kevin make the same jokes again?

SAMANTHA. Well, that's what friends do, Alison. They chill. Hang out and talk about Pokémon. Or, you know, whatever.

ALISON. Right. Small talk. Well, some people talk about real things. Things that matter.

SAMANTHA. I don't know. Maybe small talk … isn't small. Especially after something like Orlando. Or maybe the smallness is what makes it big.

ALISON. Uh huh.

SAMANTHA. Maybe it's like this big blanket that covers us. We wrap ourselves up in it.

ALISON. In the banality.

SAMANTHA. In the predictability of it. You know that Kevin's going to tell the same stupid jokes. But I kind of like that. It's a bit of home and it comforts me.

ALISON. Yeah, well, you know what would comfort me, Sam? If someone said something. A note. A phone call. A fucking post on Facebook. You know, "I'm so sorry. How are you doing? That must have been so frightening for your community." Or at least, "I can't believe all the shit that's going on." But no. Nothing. Nada. Zip.

SAMANTHA. Yeah. Well . . .

ALISON. Kevin. Rachel. Darin --- *(Samantha interrupts)*

SAMANTHA. Stop, Ally. You'll just get all worked up again.

ALISON. *(continuing, pacing now)* Laura. Michael. Michael Abbott. Michael Cunningham. Michael Rose.

SAMANTHA. *(overlapping)* Ally, *please*. Are you going to name everyone we know?

ALISON. *(overlapping, she is on a roll)* My brother. *Your* brother. My sister. Your cousin ---

SAMANTHA. Ally, *please* stop.

ALISON. For fuck's sake! It's like we don't exist. We don't exist. *(She fights back tears.)*

SAMANTHA. Of course we exist. Come here. Shhh...sweetheart...shhh. Honey, honey, honey … you have *got* to relax.

ALISON. I'm afraid. I am, Sam. And now with this maniac running for president …

SAMANTHA. Oh, you can't be serious, Alison. No one takes him seriously.

ALISON. I'm not so sure. We're in a bubble here.

SAMANTHA. We're an interracial lesbian couple in the Midwest, and you think *we're* in a bubble.

ALISON. Yeah, we're in a bubble. I mean, how much are we out in the world? Like in rural communities? Or with people that think differently than us.

SAMANTHA. Well, most people have small circles. I would rather have a few close friends.

ALISON. Oh please. A small circle that doesn't care enough to check in? What kind of *circle* is that?

SAMANTHA. Alison.

ALISON. And seriously, can we talk about what's going on? Have you seen the crowds at his rallies? There's so much hate getting stirred up.

And it's not like I feel safe in the world. I mean, do you know *any* women who really feel safe in the world? Ever??

Let alone any queers? Sometimes, I feel like a fucking target.

SAMANTHA. Like I don't? Like people are not judging *me* every day, everywhere?

ALISON. I'm sorry, babe. You're right.

SAMANTHA. But I can't, I can't function that way. I don't know. Maybe, it's just my mother speaking but you have to think positive. *We* have to look forward.

ALISON. Uh huh.

SAMANTHA. We do. Honestly, I have never seen you like this, Ally. You're scaring me. You have *got* to relax.

ALISON. But it has never been this bad as far back as I can remember. And I think it's getting worse. And I can't sleep.

SAMANTHA. I know. You kept me up half the night.

ALISON. I keep seeing their faces. So young. They had barely started their lives.

SAMANTHA. I know.

ALISON. And they go to the one place they can really be themselves. Dance. Cut loose. Cruise . . . Maybe hook up.

SAMANTHA. Yeah. I remember my first gay bar.

ALISON. Me too.

SAMANTHA. I wanted so badly to meet someone. Just to talk.

ALISON. Talk?

SAMANTHA. Ally! Yes, talk. For starters. You're so bad. I used to drive past week after week, daring myself to go in. Willing myself.

ALISON. We've all been there.

SAMANTHA. I was scared to death. Where should I look? How should I behave? What should I wear?

ALISON. You always look great, babe.

SAMANTHA. Well, *I'm* making an effort.

I know it sounds corny, but when I was coming out, well, when I finally got up the nerve *to* come out, it was like a kind of church. And you know, not exactly the kind of church I was raised in.

ALISON. Yeah. A church with a pool table. And women!

SAMANTHA. Women. *(beat)*

ALISON. I keep thinking of all their cell phones going off.

SAMANTHA. Yeah.

ALISON. *(She sings. Samantha joins her, in an effort to stay connected)*

"You used to call me on your cell phone..."

SAMANTHA. *(Remembering, singing.)*

"Cell phone..." Drake.

ALISON. I hate Drake.

SAMANTHA. What? Now you hate *Drake?*

ALISON. I don't know. I hate *this*. This, this fear, this dread. Like something is going to happen. Something terrible.

SAMANTHA. Nothing is going to happen, honey. It's over. It was horrible but it's over now.

ALISON. Who says it's over? I don't know. There could be something more. Maybe even bigger. Like this maniac running for office.

SAMANTHA. Ally. You're safe. Here. With me.

ALISON. Yeah? So why do we have to go out? *(She attempts a joke)* I mean, we already came out.

SAMANTHA. You goof. Because Kevin is expecting us.

ALISON. Oh, you know what? Fuck Kevin, Samantha. Fuck him.

SAMANTHA. Oh my God. Are you really going to do this?

ALISON. And all these so-called allies who show up at Gay Pride once a year with their little rainbow flags. They don't have a fucking clue.

SAMANTHA. That is not fair.

ALISON. Oh, really?

SAMANTHA. Kevin *is* different. He's our friend and he loves us.

ALISON. So, why nothing?

SAMANTHA. I don't know. I don't know anything anymore. I mean … Pulse. Who would have thought?

ALISON. Yeah? Well, Sandy Hook. Sandy Hook! Charleston! These men, these boys with their guns and their toxic masculinity. With their racism and their homophobia.

Sandy Hook. He shot his mother, for Christ's sake.

SAMANTHA. Yes. But what are we going to do, Ally? Write off most of the people we know? Then who is left? Seriously. You? Me? When we are far from our families? When you are scarcely speaking to yours?

ALISON. I do not want to talk about my family. You know that. Talk about homophobia.

SAMANTHA. Well, I don't want to live in a ghetto. I need our world to be bigger, more expansive. Even if some of our friends don't get it. Maybe they just don't get it yet.

ALISON. This whole conversation is making me tired.

SAMANTHA. Well, I'm tired, too.

Look, honey, maybe it's that they don't know what to say. Maybe they are just so afraid of saying the wrong thing that they don't say anything. Not because they don't care.

ALISON. Maybe.

SAMANTHA. Come on, Al, let's just see what happens at dinner tonight, please.

ALISON. And, wait to see if they bring it up?

SAMANTHA. Well, yeah. Or you could bring it up . . . .

ALISON. Oh, oh, so now it's incumbent on me to do it. To do the heavy lifting.

SAMANTHA. Ally, please. You're not the only one who is struggling. I need some normalcy around here. I need Kevin's stupid jokes and Sara's mac and cheese. And you cannot just sit and watch the same footage over and over and over again.

ALISON. Yeah, well, I can't. I just can't . . . . Maybe next week. Or . . . . next month.

SAMANTHA. But these are our friends.

ALISON. Really? A real friend would have called. Or said something on fucking Facebook. You go. You. *(Alison picks up the remote and turns the TV on again. We see and hear the same footage about the massacre. Now what?)*

The Human Traces

by Anders Lustgarten

Anders Lustgarten won the inaugural Harold Pinter Playwriting Award for his play IF YOU DON'T LET US DREAM, WE WON'T LET YOU SLEEP at the Royal Court Downstairs. LAMPEDUSA, about the migrant crisis, has been performed in thirty countries. THE SEVEN ACTS OF MERCY combined Caravaggio and austerity in the Swan Theatre at the RSC. THE SECRET THEATRE, at the Globe, is an allegory for mass surveillance set in the sixteenth century. Anders is currently writing about Israel/Palestine, the far right and mass protest among other subjects. He is also head writer on COUNTRYMEN for Viaplay/AppleTree and his first film, ALBION HOUSE, is in development with Warp/FilmFour. Prior to becoming a writer, Anders taught on Death Row in California, was an international 400m runner and was arrested in multiple continents as an activist.

What gets to you are the little things. The human traces.

I been doing this job twenty-six years in February. I seen the human body in every condition you can imagine. Insides spilled out, pieces missing, whatever. I don't wanna be graphic or upset nobody or brag on myself, I'm just telling you what it is. There's nothing about the physical reality of death that can rattle me.

It's the life that hurts. The life that was there an hour ago and now it ain't and the people never had no clue it was going. The traces of the ordinary.

Two jack and cokes on the bar with the ice cubes only half melted.

A single new white sneaker with the laces still tied.

Somebody's name and number on a napkin.

I find these things hard to take. Harder and harder, for whatever reason.

These are the first things I see when finally they let us in the club. I see them before I see the bodies, and I hope nobody takes that in a disrespectful way. But these things are still alive in some weird sense, they got human traces still quivering on 'em, and I think I might be so full up of death now that I got to cling on these traces of life whatever way I can. I like to think it's a form of tribute to these dead people I don't know from Adam and yet I'm about to handle them more intimately than their lovers, maybe even their mothers, ever did. To pay respect to the last fingerprints they left on this world. But maybe it's only for me.

Jorge don't have time for this. Jorge wants to get the bodies out and identified and reunited with their loved ones and none of my so-called 'trip-out spiritual shit' is gonna fly with him. He kicks my ass and we start lifting and shifting.

But you can shut your eyes a whole lot easier than you can shut your ears.

A cellphone starts ringing. In the back pocket of a guy in his early twenties, face down in blood. Jorge and I catch each other's eye and stop moving without meaning to. The sound echoes off the walls and bounces back at us. It rings and rings and rings, like doesn't this fucking guy have voicemail?

It stops. Jorge's shoulders drop. I take a breath. We bend the knees, squat, take a different one by the shoulders and ankles.

Another phone starts ringing.

And another.

And another.

Pretty soon it's a chorus from hell. These metallic bees buzzing round our heads, little tinny snatches of dead people's favourite songs. Ten, twelve, twenty phones are going off at once. Some ring once, twice, then stop. Some never stop. They come back and come back and come back because someone on the other end is dying inside. Screaming in terror in their souls every time nobody answers. The horror in their minds getting worse and worse and worse.

This one dude, light skinned, braids, bout my age, clean hole through his right temple, has Drake as his ringtone. "You useta call me on my cellphone," that shit. I musta heard that song thirty times. I would prefer never to hear it again.

"Somebody should answer that," I say to Jorge. Twice, because the first time he pretends not to hear me.

"Not our job," he says, not looking in my eyes. "Take that lady's feet."

"I fucking hate Drake. I can't listen to fucking Drake no more. Somebody should answer that."

"And say what?"

"Fuck would I know?"

"Take that lady's feet."

"Jorge."

"TAKE HER FEET! TAKE HER FUCKING FEET!"

We stare at each other for like ten, twenty seconds. Drake starts going again. I bend down. I take the cell phone out of the guy's pocket.

"Goddamn it, C-Los. We got work to do."

I don't even look at the name on the screen. I don't wanna know. I press the green button.

"Hello? Hello? Oh thank God. Thank you Jesus. Hello? Kevin?"

I take a deep breath and I open my mouth, without one clue what's coming out.

"I'm so so sorry to have to tell you this, but I thought you deserved to know."

There's a gasp on the other end, and a low primal moan from the gut.

From the corner of my eye, I see Jorge reaching for a phone.

GONE SILENT

by Jennifer Maisel

Jennifer Maisel is the award-winning author of many plays, among them *The Last Seder, Out of Orbit, Mallbaby, @thespeedofjake, Eight Nights,* and *Yellow Wallpaper 2.0 2020*. Her works have been seen across the US and abroad. She works extensively in film, television, web and digital dramatic media.

Contact: Jennifer Maisel

Jennifermaisel@gmail.com

ELISE

What I do is I turn my ringer off.

At night.

To sleep.

I put on the white noise app – Surf! - and I resist checking Facebook one last time.

OK, a lot of times I don't resist.

But tonight I turn my ringer off. And the surf on.

I've been trying to remember how to be less connected

Because sleep,

Sleep hasn't been what it used to be

And I've been trying to recapture what it used to be

A recharge…a reboot?

A refuge.

So I turn my ringer off because that's what they said.

The magazines and the HealthHappyApp. The doctor. My shrink.

I turn my ringer off and unconvincingly convince myself that the world of dreams is the only one that matters

I turn my ringer off and I feel Alvin's side of the bed mock me with its unrelenting emptiness

I shouldn't call it Alvin's side of the bed anymore

I turn my ringer off and I don't think of whose limbs he's entwined with now. Unsuccessfully.

I turn my ringer off and turn the white noise up

White noise waves crashing and

Loud enough to drown my own thoughts

Loud enough to carry me off to sleep.

Loud.

….

….

It isn't the noise that wakes me up.

It is the hearing nothing.

The hearing nothing.

And the screen is flooded with words and tightly sprung letters –

Mom.

Mom.

Want u to know.

We were dancing.

Anditwasloudsoloud

But the shots were louder

And I want you to know that I am ok even if I'm not ok

And the screen lights up with the photo of my beautiful complicated beautiful boy

His voice a shadow of his voice

His voice broken

Victor – he says –

He covered me and now Victor is no more than a shield Mom and Mom I never had to tell you how I loved Victor because you knew before I knew but Mom I want to make sure you know I love you -

Don't tell me that now. Tell me when you get home.

I thought you weren't going to answer and I thought I wasn't going to hear you and I thought, maybe -

My ringer. Was off.

I was on silent.

Hold tight love.

Do you think Victor knew I loved him the way you know I loved him?

Yes. We know, baby boy. We always know -

And Mom –

Silent.

Has he gone silent?

Baby boy?

Sweet boy?

I'll call back –

Don't hang up.

Don't hang up my boy.

Don't hang up sweet baby breath. I know your sweet baby breath and your puberty stink.

Crooked bottom tooth.

Birthmark on your back.

And your piercing through your right brow that you love that I hate.

Don't hang up.

Chubby melty creature turned sinewy man

Don't hang up.

But the white noise slams back into my ear

And he is carried off by the waves

And I can't call back

Because what if his ringer is on?

...

He's gone silent.

...

I keep my ringer turned on

And I wait.

I still wait.

I wait.

(OB)SCENE a monologue

by Jeff McMahon

JEFF MCMAHON: Performer/Writer whose live and media work has been presented since 1980 in the Americas, U.K. and Europe, including renowned venues The Kitchen, Dance Theater Workshop, P.S. 122, LACE, Franklin Furnace, Jacobs Pillow, and many others. Fellowships and grants: National Endowment for the Arts, NY Foundation for the Arts, NY State Council on the Arts, and more. Essays: <u>50 Key Figures In Queer US Theatre</u> (Routledge 2023), <u>Table Talk: From the Threepenny Review</u> (Counterpoint Press 2015), <u>Innovation in Five Acts: Strategies for Theatre and Performance</u> (TCG 2015), Dramatic works published in his book, <u>Six Monologues 1990-2007</u> (NoPassport Press 2018). MFA in nonfiction writing from School of the Arts, Columbia University, and BA in Interdisciplinary Art SUNY/Empire State College. Began teaching Arizona State University 2001, appointed Associate Professor 2011, Full Professor 2020, Emeritus in 2022. Writing fellow Edward F. Albee Foundation in Montauk, NY, and Fundación Valparaíso, Mojácar, Spain. Founding member of Jacki Apple Fund/Jacki Apple Award in Performance and Artist Projects.

www.jeffmcmahonprojects.net

A youngish man, somewhat unkempt, glowering

I have a presentation of sorts

A kind of gift

I am going to express myself

Here, in this nightclub [audition, theatre]

That's good, right?

"Be creative," "take the path not taken"

All that, right?

It's what my teachers said to do

I think some of you, my teachers, might be here tonight

I'd rather not hunt you down just yet

Maybe later?

You told me to just seize a moment

be expressive yet keep in control

That's theatre, the performance of self

Other people set the stage, providing props and stuff

I couldn't do it without you

We'll get to your role later

It's really all about serving the scene
I'm equipped to do that
I know the given circumstances
who, what, where, what's in my pockets and on
the dresser at home
I'm taking the responsibility of taking on a role
So now I am loading-in, marking my moves
I've cleared out the mental clutter, distractions
like family and friends
Those who would criticize me are little voices
offstage I don't hear anymore

My act will "kill"; your words
You said "metaphor" but action is God's way
You clarified, (yeah, you like words like that)

you "clarified": If there's a gun on the table in the first act…

I think the first act already happened

but maybe you fell asleep

You close your eyes sometimes when maybe you shouldn't

I can't ever close my eyes

Maybe you're tired

You run the world but I can reload while running

I have lots of arms. I'm that Hindu god guy

I don't need to ask questions and get permission

for being the canary in the coal mine up your ass

you of every color of a rainbow that always leads to the gold

but I'm not sharing

Not anymore

If you don't understand why, then you don't understand my role

I can't do the things you can

I will do the things you won't

It's in my nature to be against your nature

Me being a hunter previously lacking prey

You pray but I have to act

Once loaded I have to unload

If there's a gun on the table…

I am the shooter, that troubled teen with twenty rounds of ammo and an attitude way beneath your altitude

You didn't see me I was so low

You never cast me in the roles I wanted

I cram my emotions into containers you would call "unstable" "inappropriate" "incorrect"

I don't and never will "share"

Remember?

My "want" is retribution

and no further aspiration

You called that the refuge of the loner, the sad lot of the lost

That's the attribution you made available to me

You can't lose me now, I'm found

weaponized with a plot casting you as object not subject

A new role for you. Fewer lines.

I get the lead this time.
I didn't come here to audition.
I am the play, entire and unedited
I'll be taking the stage, unpacking my own effects. Loud sounds and bright lights. Bullets as words, a song in rounds exploding from the chamber, gaping wounds my literature though

you say I'm "illiterate." I churn burning carbon
and smother the sun, enrage the winds,
disappear trees leaving lakes of sand, garbage,
drowned potentials.
Me directing. You: cattle call

I think there's potential for a film version
but I won't be here for the residuals
Neither will you

Places please

AFTER ORLANDO

by Oliver Mayer

Oliver Mayer is playwright-librettist and professor of dramatic writing at USC in Los Angeles, California. His plays include *Blade to the Heat, Ragged Time, Ghost Waltz*, and more. For rights to this piece: Omayer@usc.edu, 310-867-9192

The bar of a nightclub, empty. A LATINA works with a mop to remove a stain on the floor that just will not go away.

A young LATINO man enters hiding under a hoodie. Looking for the bartender, he puts down a large bill on the bar.

The Latina sets the mop against the wall, takes her position as the bartender.

LATINA: Yeah?

LATINO: *(orders, whispering)* Mezcal.

He hides his face as much as possible. The drink arrives. He drinks it down in one shot. It affects him.

LATINO: *Otro.*

The second drink makes him shift his head and the hoodie falls. He is revealed to have been recently crying (though not now). He knocks it down in one shot. It affects him strongly.

LATINO: *Uno mas.* Please.

LATINA: Last call.

LATINO: This will be my last one. Promise.
He experiences a hot flash that makes him lose the hoodie completely. Taking it off, he can't help shimmying his entire body.

The Latina pours the shot, removes the bottle and returns to work on the stain with the mop, forgetting him. She goes down to her knees with a brush after the stain. Somehow he cannot drink with her on her knees. She scrubs and scrubs without effect. Eventually he joins her on the floor.

LATINO: *Disculpa*...but is that –

LATINA: Blood? No matter how hard I try, it just won't --

LATINO: May I?

She offers him her brush, but instead he pours out his mezcal.

LATINA: Pour one out? Really?

LATINO: For the homies who can't be here.

LATINA: Look!

On their knees, they stare at the floor, as something is revealed.

LATINA: Do you see them? Do you hear them? Last Call? Donna Summer's "Last Dance" as they get ready to go home alone or with friends or take a chance?

Finding themselves, some for the first time? Before they've even told their parents? Before some have even told themselves that they are *mariposon*, lesbianaut, *pajarito*, dykealicious, *maricon de playa*. Having that last sip of Moscow Mule before the ride home? Feeling free for the first time, feeling goofy, dancing on or off the beat and who gives a fuck? Being finally for once themselves....And then?

Both hear gunfire in their minds for several moments.

LATINO: I hear.

LATINA: I see.

They help each other up.

LATINO: The stain's still there.

LATINA: Of course it is. But I ain't mad at ya.

LATINO: I am. I don't know why it wasn't me.

Latino returns the empty glass to the bar, about to leave.

LATINO: It's late.

LATINA: Hold up. It ain't last call yet.

She brings the bottle over, sets it between them.

LATINA: For the homies who can't be here.

The life and times of a gay club

By Ryan Oliveira

Ryan Oliveira is a Brazilian-American playwright, dramaturg and performer. His works include Desire in a Tinier House, Soccer Player, The Queers Present: A Gender Reveal Party and Below the Pacific.

CHARACTERS:

GENN

Latinx, early 20's. A genderqueer dandy. Party-goer.

LORENA

Latina, late-40's. A cool mama visiting from out of town. Party-goer.

LUCIANO

Latino, early 30's. A casual club resident. Partygoer.

SETTING:

The ruins of a club in Orlando, FL.

TIME:

Present-day. Sunset. The kind barely closing out the day and opening up the night.

(Lights.

Sounds of a club anthem booming, as if the floor was set to epic fire.

After a moment, it slows down, as if time stops.

GENN appears, their eyes wandering at the trickling lights/sound of the space.)

GENN

First time at a gay club

After sneaking out with my friends

Not giving a fuck about my mom's high blood pressure

'Cause me dressed like this,

Acting like this is a bad example

For my straight brother who got laid in a 3some on her bed –

Fuck it.

Doesn't matter.

I'm under the sea

Watching fish in the coral,

Drinking, cleaning themselves.

Schools of 'em in the center, dancing,

Feeling themselves,

Waving their arms,

Bathing their bodies, all types of

Built and Twink and Bodies in Between

And Maybe Me.

I came miles outside the city for Maybe Me.

Like I'm comin' to the front of the church

And it's tall and Gay Gatsby the Movie and

I'm scared to admit it.

I'm scared.

(The music perks up, percolating from underwater.)

But DJ's playin' my song tonight, remixed for me.

And I got no choice but to give my body, my soul.

And it's so weird that for the first time in my life

I feel so seen.

So unseen.

I can't be unseen again.

(The music rises from the ocean. Genn is moved to dancing.)

I could be swimming my entire life.

And for my life tonight...I'm here.

(*LORENA enters, dancing.*

The music slows. Genn slows.

Lorena is laughing.)

LORENA

Another night at the gay club?

Yeah, another night!

Ain't nothin' taking me away from my boy!

Not no cancer, not no convicts,

And *especially*: No Man!

But I let my boy dance with the other guys

And he lets them dance with me.

See? I raised him right.

Gonna be a doctor someday.

Find the cure for cancer in case it comes back for me.

Third time it comes, I'll be ready.

I got my boy.

But until that day, God's gonna give me a salsa

Y Lorena is gonna get her ass a tequila sonrisa.

Porque?

I don't have to watch myself, hija!

Estoy viva and this time is too short to say

No to loving whoever the fuck you want! Mira!

(She takes her phone out and records the audience as the music perks up.

The crowd is going wild. Genn dances closer to Lorena.)

Here! Ain't nobody takin' us down!

My son, these go-gos,

These ho-hos - ain't nobody takin' us down!

(They pop confetti in the air.

The music slows as they stare at the skies, like children seeing snow for the first time.

Genn and Lorena slow-salsa in what is now a light-show of snow as LUCIANO enters.

The music reaches a bridge that slows and grows throughout, becoming more explosive as Genn and Lorena dance to match its pace.)

LUCIANO

Last night at a gay club

Fresh off my Zumba teaching

And with my boyfriend Gabe.

I'm turned thirty.

A tiny gay death.

But I got my first tattoo across my chest

And birthday sex and dinner – *duh*.

And dancing all that dining away.

(The colors in the club shimmer like a disco ball through the water's surface.)

The club was full of color,

Stained glass streaks,

Vodka tonics and sonic rumbles,

Rumbas, Reggaeton - but only flavors of it.

DJ playing the deep cuts of cumbia with Kelly Clarkson,

Even Kelly Key and Xtina.

And dancing with Gabe,

Feeling myself against his music,

Our music.

I thought, how lucky I am.

To fly out of Puerto Rico,

To find this make-up artist in Chicago,

To make a life with him in Orlando,

To condo and karaoke,

To give to people

The kind of joy in their bodies

In their souls that I feel right now.

To desire to be their best selves.

(The beat drops below the surface, and even the lights slow-dance down.)

Think of all my Facebook rants,

How gray the clouds looked living with my parents,

How blue the world was.

How everyone, everything,

Misunderstood me.

(Peeks of light pass through the surface.)

Look at all these flowers.

All these birds.

All the lovers like that Kylie Minogue video

Swaying left and right in an ocean of light.

All the sky in this club right now.

(The music begins to muffle, as if underwater. Lorena and Genn slowly break their dance. Luciano is still.)

I thank the Gabe for the love I have.

(Genn heads out in front of Luciano. Lorena holds Luciano in her arms.)

LORENA *(holding Luciano in her arms.)*

I thank God for the life I have.

(Luciano holds Genn in his arms.)

GENN

If there's a God...then I'm glad I'm here.

(They hold on tight, this club-family.
A boom - as if it was the end of the song.
Blackout. End of Play.)

The Bigger Picture

by Matthew Paul Olmos

Matthew Paul Olmos is a three-time Sundance Fellowship/Residency recipient. Affiliations: Center Theatre Group, Geffen Playhouse, Ensemble Studio Theatre, Humana Festival, New Dramatists, INTAR, New York Theatre Workshop, Oregon Shakespeare Festival. Princess Grace Awardee, La MaMa's Ellen Stewart Award (selected by Sam Shepard). Mentored by Taylor Mac & Ruth Maleczech; Kilroys nominator.
www.matthewpaulolmos.com.

a CHARISMATIC MAN talks to somebody

CHARISTMATIC MAN
Now a lotta people mistake our girl for an AR-15, cuz they got same looks, almost same build, an the sound that come out…why both sound heaven'sent.
But, as most men know, it's what goes on underneath that really matter, ain't it.
Now, our Sig Sauer MCX, she is what we like to call *compatible*, she is designed to take on a whole array of accessories; she will, in fact, *redefine* herself to whatever it is you need. No matter what the situation, no matter what the target, she will be there for you without question. That there is *gold standard*.

Now, if you open her up, what you'll see inside is what we call "gas piston technology." An what that means is, after you trigger her, the generated gas from the ignited round is pushed into a cylinder which is connected to a piston. Now you do know what a piston is, don't ya? (pause) Right, the piston is what provides the motion to eject the spent casing and chamber a fresh round. An that's what makes our girl a completely different being than the AR-15. See, people don't like to think when it comes to how to look at our

177

girls.
They just blanket, don't they?
One is just same as the other an every one look alike.
They got no idea how intricate they insides, how beautifully put their technology.
Why I bet they wouldn't like it all so very much if I were to go on television and say that all their wives was exactly the same woman, would they? Nah. Just like a man knows his wife how specific, they ought know same for these girls.

(Beat)

Now. What was it you said you wanted her for?

(Long pause)

How's that? *(pause)* No, I mean I heard ya, I just— *(pause)* Well, no, I'm happy to make you the sale, I would be remiss though if I didn't— *(pause)* Apologies, Mr. Evans— Apologies Senator.

(CHARISMATIC MAN listens intently for a few moments)

Wow. You sure do know how to speak well. I could learn a thing or two— *(pause)* Well, when you put it that way, Senator, with all that *is* happening, with our need for protection, I can see clearly how a Giveaway like the one you're putting together is truly patriotic an representative of what America is all about. Especially here in Florida.

(CHARISMATIC MAN pauses)

        CHARISMATIC MAN(cont)
So now, you're going to make the purchase and then the winner of the—

(CHARISMATIC MAN listens)

Okay, okay, so I'll set her aside for you. And try ta clean up this place for when you come back with them cameras—do *I* need to dress nice that day, I mean will *I* be on— No problem, I's just checking.
How about…signage. Will your offices be sending over any posters or displays for the Giveaway, or hell, if you want I could rustle something up myself, I got a steady hand.
(pause) No, of course, of course, online makes more sense. So I'll just…be here then. An wait for your word. Or you secretary's word.

(CHARISMATIC MAN nervously shakes somebody's hand)

And thank you Senator Evers, for thinking of the independent businessman. I appreciate being a part of something so…vital for our country.

(Beat)

Actually, before you go? I'm really just spit balling here, but…since this Giveaway is really about protection…do you think maybe a handgun, we could still do a Sig Sauer, might be a more appropriate prize?

(CHARISMATIC MAN steps back a bit, as though being scolded)

I am sorry, Senator, I did not mean to imply— your sensitivity or timing has *nothing* to do— I understand completely that you had this idea *weeks* before this unfortunate incident even—I was just thinking of practicality. How much easier it would be for an everyday citizen to arm themselves with something…easier to carry, is all. I apologize for not seein'the big picture of things the way that you do—

(Sound of somebody exiting a store)

Oh. Okay then. So…I'll be here for you, I'll be waiting for your word…been meaning to clean this store up anyways, so…this'll give me a reason then…

(Lights fade on CHARISMATIC MAN looking for hope outside his door.
END OF PLAY)

THE SEA A CHORAL POEM

By Giovanni Ortega

This Choral Poem was written on June 15, 2016 immediately after the PULSE was taken.

Giovanni Ortega recently finished *The Pinoy Trilogy: The Butterfly of Chula Vista* (San Diego Rep), *Criers for Hire* (EWP) & of *ALLOS*. He also devised *The Body Series* at the Haque Centre in Singapore. The shows have been presented in the U.S. and Australia, where he was a resident scholar for Playwriting Australia's National Play Festival. Additional works: National Poetry Festival Singapore - *Benches (2017), Palindromes (2018), Belonging (2019) & Contour (2020). Goddess of Mt. Banahaw, El Pescador y La Lluvia* and *Fugaz de La Piel Canela – Fleeting Cinnamon Skin*. He is the author of "Leaves from the Silverlake Barrio," "Ang Gitano" (Carayan Press) and various Climate Change Play anthologies including "Where is the Hope" and " Lighting the Way" as well as "Completely Mixed Up: Mixed Heritage Writing and Art." Giovanni is an Assistant Professor in Pomona College's Department of Theatre for the Claremont Colleges.

PLAYWRIGHT'S NOTE:

The sensitivities of this incident especially with the Queer POC community should be taken into consideration when presenting the Choral Poem. We, as Queer POC continue to navigate the balance of marginalization between racial, religious and queer identity within our communities.

CHARACTERS:

EM – An Individual

SEA – An Individual

ECH – An Individual

P1 – PERSON 1 (Person of Color)

G1 – GROUP 1 (People of Color)

P2- PERSON 2

G2 – GROUP 2

STAGE DIRECTIONS:

Three people enter on different sides of the stage, creating the edges of a triangle.

They start reciting in a whisper and following the rituals that correspond with each prayer. Their words are simultaneously spoken throughout the Poem until they join the Chorus.

LIGHTS UP:

EM

Bismillah hir rahman nirahim (In the name of Allah, the most beneficent, the most merciful). Alhamdulillah hir Rabbil Alaameen◉Ar-rahman nir-raheem.◉Mal(ee)ki Yo Mid-deen.◉Ea-yaka nabudu wa iyya-ka nastaeen.◉Ih dinas siratal mustaqim◉Siratal ladzina an amta alayhim◉Ghayral magh doobey alayhim◉Wala daa leen◉Ameen.

SEA

Dios te salve, María, llena eres de gracia,

el Señor es contigo.

Bendita tú eres entre todas las mujeres,

y bendito es el fruto de tu vientre, Jesús.

Santa María, Madre de Dios,

ruega por nosotros pecadores,

ahora y en la hora de nuestra muerte.

ECH

Yitgadal v'yitkadash sh'mei raba.

B'alma di v'ra chirutei,

v'yamlich malchutei,

b'chayeichon uv'yomeichon

uv'chayei d'chol beit Yisrael,

baagala uviz'man kariv. V'im'ru: Amen.

Y'hei sh'mei raba m'varach

l'alam ul'almei almaya.

Yitbarach v'yishtabach v'yitpaar

v'yitromam v'yitnasei,

v'yit'hadar v'yitaleh v'yit'halal

sh'mei d'kud'sha b'rich hu,

l'eila min kol birchata v'shirata,

tushb'chata v'nechemata,

daamiran b'alma. V'imru: Amen.

Y'hei sh'lama raba min sh'maya,

v'chayim aleinu v'al kol Yisrael.

V'imru: Amen.

Oseh shalom bimromav,

Hu yaaseh shalom aleinu,

v'al kol Yisrael. V'imru: Amen.

GLBTTQI and non-gender binary characters walk onstage one by one throughout the whole piece. The chorus should start and end with a person of colour.

P1

A pain as immense as the sea.

We will not fade into darkness.

We will be seen.

G1

Our race includes all colors, religions, social class, genders - conforming or not.

A race that will take you into the depths and alleyways of the streets

and the successes of Power and Pride amidst prejudice.

G2

A race watching the next generation of our kin

to ensure that they don't experience what we went through,

so that they are not censored and brought back into persecution for who they love and what they are.

P2

Because our race knows what it's like to be in hiding.

To be spat on, to be excluded, laughed at and hated.

G1 & G2

Our race; once the secret society hiding in closets and songs feeling alive when we gather from dusk till dawn where we speak in tongues and code switch in silence,

now an emblem of survival.

EM, SEA & ECH

Crying in each other's arms because we were called......

Shouting in Sadness because s/he/they were exiled again.

Screaming in angst because we lost another one,

another 10, another 100, another 1,000.

P1

No one can erase our race.

G2

We take care of the elderly grandmother

the abandoned sister

the lost drug addicted friend

the family business

the cousin needing a ride home after a brawl with her man.

the confused colleague.

the grieving mother

G1 & G2

We are the race that will make you laugh and cry at the same time

when you feel alone, abandoned and lost in the sky.

We will tell you to fly.

EM, SEA & ECH

It's no longer a secret.

G1 w/ EM, SEA & ECH

From Orlando, Malaysia, Manila, Tehran to Abuja Nigeria

From Bogotá, Lima, Istanbul, Birminghan to Lafayette Louisiana.

ALL

Our Family.

A pain as immense as the sea.

We will not fade into darkness. We will be seen.

P1

Vamos a vivir, mi familia.

Lumipad Ka.

Fly.

The chorus members leave, EM, SEA & ECH go back to their prospective areas and continue their prayers without the rituals.

LIGHTS FADE

TRANSLATION:

I.

Bismillah hir rahman nirahim

Alhamdulillah hir Rabbil Alaameen☉Ar-rahman nir-raheem.☉

Mal(ee)ki Yo Mid-deen.☉

Ea-yaka nabudu wa iyya-ka nastaeen.☉

Ih dinas siratal mustaqim☉Siratal ladzina an amta alayhim☉

Ghayral magh doobey alayhim☉Wala daa leen☉Ameen.

In the name of Allah, the compassionate, the merciful.

All praise is for Allah, the Rabb (Lord) of the worlds.

The compassionate the merciful.

Master of the Day of Judgment.

You alone we worship and You alone we call on for help.

Guide us to the right way.

The way of those whom You favored; not those who have earned Your wrath, or of those who have lost the way.

Amen.

II.

Dios te salve, María, llena eres de gracia,

el Señor es contigo.

Bendita tú eres entre todas las mujeres,

y bendito es el fruto de tu vientre, Jesús.

Santa María, Madre de Dios,

ruega por nosotros pecadores,

ahora y en la hora de nuestra muerte.

Hail Mary, full of grace,

the Lord is with thee.

Blessed art thou among women,

and blessed is the fruit of thy womb, Jesus.

Holy Mary, Mother of God,

pray for us sinners,

now and at the hour of our death.

Amen.

III.

Yitgadal v'yitkadash sh'mei raba.

B'alma di v'ra chirutei,

v'yamlich malchutei,

b'chayeichon uv'yomeichon

uv'chayei d'chol beit Yisrael,

baagala uviz'man kariv. V'im'ru: Amen.

Y'hei sh'mei raba m'varach

l'alam ul'almei almaya.

Yitbarach v'yishtabach v'yitpaar

v'yitromam v'yitnasei,

v'yit'hadar v'yitaleh v'yit'halal

sh'mei d'kud'sha b'rich hu,

l'eila min kol birchata v'shirata,

tushb'chata v'nechemata,

daamiran b'alma. V'imru: Amen.

Y'hei sh'lama raba min sh'maya,

v'chayim aleinu v'al kol Yisrael.

V'imru: Amen.

Oseh shalom bimromav,

Hu yaaseh shalom aleinu,

v'al kol Yisrael. V'imru: Amen.

Exalted and hallowed be God's great name

in the world which God created, according to plan.

May God's majesty be revealed in the days of our lifetime

and the life of all Israel -- speedily, imminently, to which we say Amen.

Blessed be God's great name to all eternity.

Blessed, praised, honored, exalted, extolled, glorified, adored, and lauded

be the name of the Holy Blessed One, beyond all

earthly words and songs of blessing,

praise, and comfort. To which we say Amen.

May there be abundant peace from heaven, and life, for us and all Israel,

to which we say Amen.

May the One who creates harmony on high, bring peace to us and to all Israel.

To which we say Amen.

Today is a Good Day

After Orlando

By Katie Pearl

Katie Pearl is a director, playwright and educator. Her work explores the performance event as a tool for engagement, one that can spark flexibility of thought, build trust in imagination, and enliven people to the world and to each other, . She is the Co-Artistic Director of the interdisciplinary company PearlDamour, a company she shares with fellow theater maker Lisa D'Amour. Her work has been supported by the NEA, the MAP fund, and Creative Capital, along with other regional organizations. Pearl teaches directing and devising atWesleyan University. katiepearl@gmail.com

This is a tribute to the people killed at Pulse in Orlando.

49 people fill the space.
Each wears headphones.
Each listens to their favorite dance music on their headphones. GO.
They dance 3 minutes to the music they are listening to.

During those 3 minutes, there is the following text.
The text can appear via projection.
The text can be spoken by the dancers.
The text can be spoken by a person or persons observing the dancers.
The text can be whispered in the ears of the audience.
The text can exist in the minds of the dancers.
The audience can read the text aloud.

It's really up to you.

These 3 minutes should be exactly the way you want them to be.

Each detail in the litany below is taken from one of their obituaries,

as published in the Orlando Sentinel.

*

Today is a good day to bubble up and get down.

Today is a good day to live with your pet Chihuahuas.

Today is a good day to have a personal renaissance.

Today is a good day to get everyone into peanut butter.

Today is a good day to be a kind boss.

Today is a good day to belt out Beyoncé. To blast the music. To make everyone laugh. Today is a good day to spread love.

Today is a good day to study to be a nurse. Today is a good day to donate blood.

Today is a good day to work your way up.

Today is a good day to cook the best. To Keep friends and family close.

Today is a good day to call someone at night and tell them their favorite food is on sale at the supermarket ("Dude, your favorite food is on sale at the supermarket!!!")

Today is a good day to give advice.

Today is a good day to poke fun at yourself.

Today is a good day to find your joy on a dance floor.

Today is a good day to have a whole conversation in a parking lot.

Today is a good day to teach your kid sister to walk on

heels.

Today is a good day to coordinate the first---ever gay cruise to Cuba. To go to gay days at Walt Disney. To go to prom on your own.
To be smitten with Beyoncé.
Today is a good day to wear make up and be a man.

Today is a good day to text your mother you love her ("mommy I love you").

Today is a good day to tattoo your life philosophy on your upper right arm ("love has no gender").

Today is a good day to give more than you get. To make money and send some home. To hang out at the bear den. To plan your son a Ferrari---themed party.

Today is a good day to start to chart your own life.
Today is a good day to raise 11 children, to run a tight ship, to do what you love and dance.

Today is a good day to find love at the perfume counter.

Today is a good day to leave Hawaii to be with your mom. To shape your own father. To pose for a photo with a wax figure of Selena Gomez.

Today is a good day to find comfort in your husband's spirit, to raise $4000 to give your son the funeral he deserves, to work a double shift if you have to, to be part of two families.

Today is a good day to buy your first house.

Today is a good day to be adored by your mother,

Today is a good day to take your son swimming.

Today is a good day to fancy St. Bernard's, to produce a kids talent show. create costumes for the pageant, make someone feel beautiful while cutting their hair.

Today is a good day to marry a race car driver.

Today is a good day to lead the way with your smooth voice.

Today is a good day to run the Harry Potter ride.

Today is a good day to stroll into a life, quietly and change the way it's lived.

Today is good day to buy a bottle of Declaration by Cartier.

Today is a good day to be proud to be a Latino.

Today is a good day to love him the moment you meet him. (Tell Jesus to step up his salsa game.)

'Til the DJ Quits Playing

By Brian Quijada

Brian Quijada is an actor, playwright, and composer whose original work has been produced at Victory Gardens, Teatro Vista, Ensemble Studio Theatre, The Kennedy Center, Boise Contemporary, 1st Stage, City Theatre Pittsburgh, Geva Theatre, and Actors Theatre of Louisville. He is a proud member of The Ensemble Studio Theatre.

A young Latino man stands on stage.

I can't tell you how many weddings, quinceañeras, baptism parties I've been to in my lifetime.

My parents always forced me to go.

As kids we just used those times as play dates,

runnning around the reception hall playing tag, hide and seek, while the adults all drank and danced.

I never understood it.

Dancing to me, seemed boring. Contrived.
Constricted to a section of the room, a dance floor, lit up by tacky colored lights.

I never liked dancing.

I was never really good at it.

Always made me feel awkward.

Like everyone was staring and whispering to eachother about how I dumb I look.

So as I got older,

the parties got more boring.

I wasn't a kid anymore.

A teenager making small talk with old family members,

until the party always, inevitably focused on the dancing.

It's how Latinos do it.

They dance 'til the DJ quits playing.

But I remember one time,

I had to have been like 14 or 15,

The DJ shouted, "Que comiense la fiesta!"

and the music started blasting.

And so I just sat there watching as the dance floor was flocked by friends and relatives.

I sat on the sidelines. Like always.

And after a few songs, a girl who I didn't know approached me.

She was about my age.

I didn't know who she was but she reached out her hand and asked me to dance.

I immediately said no.

Now at the time I was confused about my attraction to boys, and what it meant to dance with girls or boys, but it wasn't that that made me say no so quick. I just didn't want to dance and was terrified of looking like a fool.

And she asked, "Are you sure?"

…

Was I sure?

And right then, it's like she looked into my soul, and asked me, "What are you so afraid of?"

And I replied, "yes. I'm sure."

She said ok, and danced right back onto the floor.

That night, I watched her dance with everyone.

Girls, boys, adults, kids.

Dance like no one was watching.

It was glorious.

I couldn't stop smiling. Her joy was infectious.

Towards the end of the night,

we caught eyes, I mean she noticed me staring at her dancing, and she motioned for me to get up and dance.

By that point everybody was pretty drunk and nobody was really paying any attention to anything.

So, I said, "what the hell!" I got up… and I. danced. my little heart out.

"Own it!" That's what the girl kept shouting at me!

(Laughs)

"Own it!"

"No one can stop you!" She shouted as we danced!

And it felt amazing.

It must've looked like I was having a seizure on the dance floor I was having such a blast.

We made a giant circle and people took turns dancing in the middle.

And when my turn came up, I threw myself onto the floor and just started thrusting to the beat of the music.

I felt it.

The joy. The "Here I am" of it all. And it wasn't about anybody. It was just everybody.

I felt free. Included in something greater.

And I didn't have any "actual" moves per say, but I was moved.

That one night felt like the beginning for me.

I never saw that girl again, but I'll never forget her.

She helped me… come out, in a way.

She reached out the idea that I don't need to be afraid.

Of being judged, mocked… of being myself.

So now I dance.

In my own way. I shake what my momma gave me.

I go to clubs where I feel accepted and feel free to mingle.

Where the DJ spins til we drop. Til the DJ quits playing,

I dance.

I own it.

And no one can stop me.

No matter what.

Sauce

by Sung Rno

Sung Rno's plays include *wAve, Yi Sang Counts to Thirteen, Cleveland Raining, Happy, Galois* (musical), *Sophocles in Staten Island* and *Boxer Rebellion*. As NEA/TCG fellow with Ma-Yi Theater, founded Ma-Yi Writers' Lab; NYC Fringe Best Play award; Helen Merrill Playwriting Fellowship. BA, Harvard; MFA, Brown; New Dramatists Alum.

"Some Chick fil A employees in Orlando showed up for work on Sunday, departing from the normal hours the fast food chain keeps in order to prepare food for first responders and people donating blood to victims of the shooting at gay nightclub Pulse."
-USA Today

A pool of light: GINA, a young worker in a Chik fil A uniform is stacking boxes of chicken and adding different packets of sauces into each box.

GINA

I didn't really know what to do

When I heard

I felt like

I felt

I don't

I don't know

I don't know what I felt to be honest

I don't know if there is a proper word for it

One thing I noticed in the morning. The silence. Eerie. So quiet. Still. So deathly quiet. The sun was shining. If you didn't know it would have seemed like any Sunday. The air was so still so horrible so beautiful so sad. And if you saw anyone on the street, you didn't feel like you needed to say anything. Or that you could. So it was quiet in this pure way. Something you felt in your bones. Like we were all just existing in this one moment together.

Someone said to pray for Orlando. I don't know if prayer is enough anymore. We pray for Boston. We pray for Paris. We pray for California. For Sandy Hook. For Parkland. Now we don't even remember the places. Because you lose count. But then what do we do anyway? We go back to our daily lives. We get a little more numb. Someone has chipped away again at our basic ability to feel. We need more than a hashtag…but what? I'm not a doctor. I'm not a detective. What do I do? I make chicken. Or chikin, as we spell it. Now, mind you, our chicken is the best in the world. People drive over 2 hours just to have a taste. Last year our whole company sold enough sandwiches to circle the world — that is a whole lot of chicken. So I called up my boss George —

GEORGE (APPEARS IN LIGHT, ON PHONE)
Yeah?

GINA
It's Gina. I think we should open up the store.

GEORGE
Did you not hear the news?

GINA
That's why we should. They're giving blood. They'll need food.

GEORGE

You know we don't open on Sundays.

GINA

You're going to talk about RULES right now?

GEORGE

Calm down, it's just our company values.

GINA

What does our company value?

GEORGE

(Beat.)

Let me think about it. Don't do anything until I call you.

GINA

What am I gonna do?

GEORGE

I know you.

(George hangs up. Lights out on him.)

GINA

I tried to not do anything. But I had to do something. So I got on the road and just started driving. And then everything suddenly got so hollow, like I was falling into this liquid sinkhole. After driving around in a trance, I realized I was here in the parking lot. I just sat in the car staring out at the empty parking lot. I have an extra key, so why not? I turned on the lights, started heating up the oil. I mean it's just another piece of chicken, right? Like you go to the bar and just you want another drink. And when the music is on and you feel the beat, you just want another song. When I go dancing with my friends, I always like to stay to the last song. The really good DJ's, they know how to build to that moment. They bring you up and then slow it down. They build up that anticipation. That longing. That joy. Because you want that last song to carry you into the night. You want it to stay in your heart. My friend Luis and I would always dance until that last song. Because the last song…it lingers…it lives on inside of you…and in that moment, as the beat consumes your every being, time stops…

You know what I get asked about most? Our special sauce. People always ask me what the secret ingredient is. It was actually a mistake. Some guy running one of the first Chik fil A's just accidentally mixed barbecue sauce into the honey mustard sauce and people started to love it. That sauce just happened. By chance. Just like why do you end up at a certain place at a certain time? Why am I here this very moment?

People originally thought the shots were part of the song. They thought it was the drum and bass. To a Ying Yang song or something.

Ying. Yang.

Drum. Bass.

Shot. Drum.

Bass. Shot.

You know the real key to the secret sauce? It's not just the barbecue sauce. Or the honey and mustard. Or the touch of mayo. Or the lime juice. You know what it is?

Shot. Drum. Shot. Bass.

Drum. Shot. Bass. Shot.

Drum. Bass. Love. Shot.

Drum. Bass. Love. Love.

Drum. Love. Love. Love.

It's what you bring from your heart. When you mix it all together.

(She holds out the box of chicken, with a packet of sauce.)

I made this for you.
Please, have some.
It really is the best. Especially when it's made for someone.
Please. It's for you.

(She bravely smiles. Still extending the box to the audience…

        Lights fade.)

        ***

Orlando

By Elaine Romero

Elaine Romero, an award-winning U.S. playwright, plays have been produced across the U.S. and abroad. Widely commissioned and published, she recently completed a war pentalogy and a border trilogy. Romero is an Associate Professor in the School of Theatre, Film, and Television at the University of Arizona and the Playwright-in-Residence at Arizona Theatre Company. In March 2021, RomeroFest featured her work internationally.

Contact:

Gurman Agency
Susan Gurman
14 Penn Plaza, Suite 1703
917 640 7027
New York, NY 10122-1701
www.elaineromero.com
212 749 4618
susan@gurmanagency.com

CHARACTERS

ORLANDO — Latina. Her gown flows like the Statue of Liberty's would if she were here.

CHORUS — They were at Pulse. People of the Global Majority. A spectrum of life.

TIME: Present

LOCATION: Orlando

PLACE: Where the living meet the dead.

ORLANDO

Orlando faces her denizens. She walks among them. They walk in her. It is a sacred relationship. Sometimes it's hard to see where she begins and they end, as it should be between a place and her people.

ORLANDO
I AM A CITY.

CHORUS
We are your city.

Tucson

Las Vegas

Orlando

Our names are not a synonym for death.

ORLANDO
I am Orlando.

My name is not a synonym for death.

CHORUS
Our names are not a synonym for death.

ORLANDO
My dead are not a synonym for tragedy.

CHORUS
Our lives are not a synonym for tragedy.

ORLANDO
Their dance is not a synonym for sin.

CHORUS
Our dance is not a synonym for sin.

ORLANDO
Their love is not a synonym for crime.

CHORUS
Our love is not a synonym for crime.

ORLANDO
There are no synonyms here.

CHORUS
We are not synonyms.

ORLANDO
Only people

CHORUS
Only us

ORLANDO
In the end.

CHORUS
In the end.

ORLANDO
In the end.

I breathe in the people

who walk on my back.

CHORUS
We walk on your back.

ORLANDO
On the inhale

they tell me their pain.

CHORUS
We tell you our pain.

ORLANDO
On the exhale

I listen to their joy.

CHORUS
We share our joy.

ORLANDO
On the inhale

I host the living

CHORUS
We live.

ORLANDO
On the exhale

I bury my dead

CHORUS
We die.

ORLANDO
But we will breathe again.

CHORUS
We will breathe.

ORLANDO
Again.

CHORUS
Again.

ORLANDO
We will breathe again.

CHORUS
Such breath.

In memory

and in truth

ORLANDO
I am a city.

I am a city.

I am your city.

CHORUS
We are your city.

We are your city.

We are your city.

ORLANDO
I am not a news story.

CHORUS
You are not a news story.

ORLANDO
I am not a news story.

CHORUS
We are not your news story.

ORLANDO
I am not a pang in your heart.

CHORUS
We are not a pang in your heart.

ORLANDO
I am not your shorthand

CHORUS
We are not your shorthand

ORLANDO
for hate

CHORUS
for hate

ALL
We are not your shorthand

ORLANDO
for unspeakable acts

CHORUS
for unspeakable acts

ORLANDO
for the way you choose to remember

how someone dies

CHORUS
how we die

ORLANDO
instead of how

CHORUS
We live

ORLANDO
I am not a synonym for that.

For reduction

Of the name of a city.

Of the span of a human life.

CHORUS
Of the span of my human life.

ORLANDO
Of the breadth of a human heart.

CHORUS
Or the breadth of my human heart.

ORLANDO
I am no synonym for truncated things.

CHORUS
for truncated things.

ORLANDO
I am your city.

I am your city.

ALL
We are your city.

ORLANDO
I live.

I live.

CHORUS
We live.

ORLANDO
I am Orlando.

CHORUS
We are Orlando.

Dance On... (In honour of the forty nine)

By Ian Rowlands

Ian Rowlands is a Welsh playwright and director.

Ian.rowlands@mail.com

N.B. For the reconfiguration of the text, I am indebted to the audio recording made by Calaghan Sgogman and Natalia Lava Lesgala whilst student at USC.

TWO PEOPLE READ

A

I am a playwright, but this is no play

B

Stanley Manolo Almodóvar III

A

I won't ask to be released by you at the end. I'm no Prospero. To be released is to be asbsolved, to forget. I can't forget. How dare I forget

B

Amanda Alvear, Oscar Aracena-Montero

A

You know, when I first heard the news, saw your pictures; the diagrams of where you'd all been killed in that club, corner of Kaley Street and South Orange Avenue, I thought of my own clubbing days

B

Rodolfo Ayala-Ayala, Antonio Davon Brown

A

Dark walls, bright lights. I haven't been in a club for years. My clubbing time was the time of Sylvester. He made us all feel *Mighty Real*. The scent of sweat and amyl nitrate; the pulsing beats of those times. So much.... joy. I imagined you enjoying, as much as I used to enjoy, in the moment before...

B

Darryl Roman Burt II, Angel L. Candelario-Padró

A

Yeah, when I first heard the news, I had this vision of you all dancing in a moment of ecstasy, of youth, in love, full of promise. Were you a dervish on that dance floor?

B

Juan Chevez-Martinez

A

Were you? And then I thought of Manhattan, a world away from Orlando, but the world is small. Once, walking down Broadway... Did you ever walk down Broadway?

B

Luis Daniel Conde

A

Did you? Mm? Well I was walking down Broadway one morning and it'd just been raining and the air had that empty feeling it has after a storm. It carries sound in a different way. You know that way?

B

Cory James Connell

A

Sound hangs in emptied air, longer than it should. Anyway, I was walking past Union Square when I heard what I thought was chanting; and the sound drew me in

B

Tevin Eugene Crosby

A

And there, on a platform, two people were standing in front of microphones. Just standing and reading

B

Deonka Deidra Drayton

A

No drama in their voices, no pretension, just reading, quietly in turn. The first person read one name

B

Simon Adrian Carrillo Fernandez

A

The second, read another

B

Leroy Valentín Fernández

A

Then the first person read again

B

Mercedez Marisol Flores

A

And this went on and on; all the names of all the people who'd died of Aids in Manhattan over the years. Each name read out tenderly, with respect, with rememberance

B

Peter O. González-Cruz, Juan Ramon Guerrero, Paul Terrell Henry, Frank Hernández, Miguel Angel Honorato

A

And I stood there in Union Square mesmerised by the names of people I would never meet; horrified by the indiscrimitae taking away of so much fabulous beauty before its time. Name after name after name

B

Javier Jorge-Reyes, Jason Benjamin Josaphat

A

I never imagined the simple reading of names could be so dignified; so dramatic. But it was no drama, no mirror to life, it was all too *Mighty Real* for that; beyond any imagining

B

Eddie Jamal Droy Justice

A

Each name a pulse, a heart beat, beating still

B

Anthony Luis Laureanodisla, Christopher Andrew Leinonen

A

Yeah, when I first heard of the tragedy of Orlando, I though of Manhattan and pictured you dancing

B

Alejandro BarriosMartínez, Brenda Lee Marquez McCool, Gilberto Ramon Silva Menéndez,, Kimberly Morris

A

Dancing

B

Akyra Monet Murray

A

You are not dead

B

Luis Omar Ocasio-Capo, Geraldo A. Ortiz-Jimenez

A

You are not dead whose names can be read and remembered

B

Eric Ivan Ortiz-Rivera, Joel Rayon Paniagua, Jean Carlo Mendez Perez, Enrique L. Rios Jr.

A

You are not dead, and this is no play

B

Jean C. Nieves Rodríguez, Xavier Emmanuel Serrano Rosado,

A

It is a pulse, the eternal beat of you; the forty nine who danced in Orlando that night

B

Christopher Joseph Sanfeliz, Yilmary Rodriguez Solivan, Edward Sotomayor Jr.

A

And still dance on

B

Shane Evan Tomlinson, Martin Benitez Torres, Jonathan Antonio Camuy Vega, Luis S. Vielma, Franky Jimmy De Jesús Velázquez, Juan P. Rivera Velázquez, Luis Daniel Wilson-León, Jerald Arthur Wright...

AFTER (a kinda litany or something)

by Riti Sachdeva

RITI is a performance maker and cultural worker, Riti Sachdeva has been creating art in some shape or rhythm for over 25 years. Incorporating text, installation, song, and dance into her writing and performance, she straddles the practices of traditional U.S. theater, performance art, and international theater forms. Interweaving the personal, political, and arcane, she has crafted the singular *Indo-Gothic* aesthetic of her work.

CASTING: *Seven characters. At least four actors are needed. Double if needed.*

NOTE: *This piece is like polyrhythmic music. Play with different tones, pitches, tempos.*

A
After, I smoked a joint.

B
After, I fucked his brains out.

C
After, I went to church.

D
After, I wanted to go jogging… but… my knees wouldn't bend. So I just sat there. Watching.

E
After, I listened to *Sabor A Mi*… but… I couldn't taste it.

F
After, I got up and made the meal we would all eat before sunrise… but… no one ate.

D
After, I watched every news channel, ABC, NBC, CBS, CNN, FOX. Five news channels that kept

showing the same footage, playing the same audio, over and over and over/

G
After, I saw his picture and thought, "He looks like my brother. Like the kid who set off the bomb at the Boston marathon. They look like my brother. So many of these guys... look like/

E
After, I called my best friend to see if she was okay cuz she loves to salsa and she was on vacation down there and she had sent me a text that said, "Mami needs to mingle..."

A
After, he went to the frig and pulled out a beer, drained it. Then he went back to the frig, pulled out a beer, drained it. In the course of three hours, he did this ten times.

B
After, I thought the best revenge would be the best fuck ever. Pulled out a tube of lube and department of public health issued condoms and went to work on him. When I'm fucking him, you can't tell if he's Latino or Muslim or both.

C
After, we prayed for their souls even though we knew they were going to burn in hell for their sins. On account of being sinners. On account of being homosexuals. And Catholics.

D
And I had the same feeling I did after September 11. Seeing it over and over and over again. It's really too much to bear. I mean, what the fuck can anyone really do after watching it, hearing it, watching it, hearing it, watching it, hearing it. It either makes you wanna climb under the covers or pull out a gun and go after them.

G
My brother could pass for some ethnic white guy, I guess. He's clean shaven, untanned. He looks like them, but we're not Arab or Muslim or anything but wow, when I see the pictures of those guys, sometimes I think I should go through my brother's closet when he's not home just to make sure…

E
I was like, "go do yo thang, mami, and post it on Instagram so I could see all them honeys you minglin wit." The posts stopped at about 1:45 in the morning. My call went to her voicemail which wasn't set up anyways. They all did. All the calls just keep going to her voicemail.

A
It scares me how much he drinks. Before and after. It's not like he was connected at all to what happened but just living in this world. Cops shoot black boys, fraternity boys rape young women, drones blow up old ladies picking vegetables, children drown escaping extremists, little boys are turned into killers, little girls are turned into hookers. I don't know why I don't drink, too.

B
That's right. I grieve by fucking. If those motherfuckers hate assfuckers then I'm gonna fuck assholes til my dick falls off.

C
I know those Islamics are sinners too, but it's strange how sinners sometimes do God's work without even knowing it. I mean, I know they think they're doing God's work but they actually really are…

F
No one ate a thing. It's better not to if you're going to be tortured. And given what just happened, we figured we should prepare for the worst.

The End (for now)

Could You Love Me?

by Madeline Sayet

Madeline Sayet is a Mohegan theater maker who believes the stories we pass down inform our collective possible futures. For her work as a theater maker she has been honored as a Forbes 30Under30, TED Fellow, and recipient of The White House Champion of Change Award from President Obama. Her plays include *Where We Belong, Up and Down the River, Antigone Or And Still She Must Rise Up, Daughters of Leda, The Neverland*, and *The Fish*. She is a Clinical Associate Professor at ASU, with the Arizona Center for Medieval and Renaissance Studies (ACMRS), and the Executive Director of the Yale Indigenous Performing Arts Program (YIPAP). www.madelinesayet.com

Representation: Michael Finkle, WME
MFinkle@wmeagency.com 212.903.1144

COULD YOU LOVE ME?

Love me? Could you? Yes you. Could you love me?

I wish I was talking to someone else, believe me.

You frighten me.

But I have to talk to you.

You're here. I'm here.

So.

I need you.

I need you to love me. Can you do that?

It's quite simple really.

Can you love me enough to save me?

I can smell your sweat. Tears. Blood. Pressed against my senses.

I'm drowning in it.

We are all salt water. Waiting to find out what form we will take.

The pressure of who we are sucks the oxygen from the room.

Dance with me?

Salt. Sweat. Tears. Blood.

Two big fears. Wanna know em?

One is being left alone.

Two - the eyes of my grandmothers if they found out who I am.

Eyes. Their eyes. That's all.

That's enough.

Imagining.

Their eyes.

The weight of so many generations of ancestors - disappointed?

Ghosts I want to believe will love me

Stop looking for it. Love. Give it up.

Hate

If they find out who I am

People will hate

The whole world around me will shift.

Change.

Tears. Sweat. Blood.

I am not ready

What form?

The past. We're not past that.

I want to feel safe. Be loved.

Will I ever be ready?

To stand bare in front of someone else waiting to be judged.

To stand bare in front of myself.

Alone in a house. Naked. Alone with a gun. Exposed. I want it. Sweat. It wants me. I cannot think. Inching to the edge of the subway platform - dark thoughts consume me. Blood. Bad medicine. It wants me. It wants my - tears. My -

Blood. The history of people who say I shouldn't exist.

Sweat. Homes filled with arms where death lurks in every corner.

Tears. Streets filled with arms. Are any of us safe?

Death wants me more than life and has no gender. No race. No history.

We are all salt water.

If it was me or you - who would live?

My self-loathing or your remorse

I like to think I will be ok.

That I will love myself enough.

But I want you to be ok too.

Can we share kindness?

Who decides which children take up arms

Against themselves

No war is winnable

Death wants us all

I will love you

More than killing's lust

More than distrust

I will love you

Are you more vulnerable with a gun or without one?

Can you love me enough to save me?

I want poetry and action

I have fear and mistakes. - We are the same.

Maybe a gun in my hand. Makes me safer. Who does it threaten?

Could you love me?

I am asking you to save my life.

Look at me. Really look.

Can you see my sweat? Touch my heart. Kiss my tears?

Would you rather kill someone else than save yourself?

Where does the gun in my hand go if I misfire?

Ricochet.

Who do you trust more - my bullets or me?

Always afraid. Ricochet. Where will the bullets go?

I am. Still here.

Love me enough to save me. Before you drown in salt.

Before. Before. After.

A Memory Play After Orlando

By Lisa Schlesinger

Lisa Schlesinger is a playwright/writer/theatre activist. Her works are performed internationally and published by American Theatre Magazine, Performing Arts Journal, Theater Magazine, The American Theatre Reader, Broadway Plays, No Passport, and the New York Times. She is co-head of the Iowa Playwrights Workshop at the University of Iowa.

Contact:
Charlotte Knight
Knight Hall Agency
Lower Ground Floor,
7 Mallow Street, London, EC1Y 8RQ
Telephone+44 (0) 20 3397 2901
office@knighthallagency.com

Characters

Monique

Valentina

Young women playing themselves as girls of about 14.

Loud club music. Valentina and Monique dance.

Lights shift and silence. They freeze, then.

MONIQUE
Before.

With each before *she taps Valentina on the head.*

Before.
Before.
After!

Monique runs around Valentina. At After! Valentina stands and runs around the little circle after her. But it's silly because the circle is so small. Valentina taps her and they stop.

VALENTINA

Again.

She sits as before. They play again. As before.

MONIQUE

Before.
Before
Before.
After!

They run as before until Valentina taps her. They look at each other some moments.

VALENTINA
Again.

MONIQUE
No.

VALENTINA
Why not?

MONIQUE
Because it is after. It's not before. Let's stop pretending.

VALENTINA
Okay.

They look at the audience. They are too still.

Let's *act* like it is before.

MONIQUE
Okay.

VALENTINA
What do we do?

MONIQUE
You know.

VALENTINA
What?

MONIQUE
You know. Do it. You did it before.

VALENTINA
I can't remember. I can never remember what I *acted like* before.

MONIQUE
You have to.

VALENTINA
I can't. Tell me.

MONIQUE
Be me. Act like me.

VALENTINA
Ok. I'll be you. Now what.

MONIQUE
Stand here.

VALENTINA
Now what.

MONIQUE
Before

She taps her on the head.

Before.

She taps her Again.

Before.

Again.

After!

Monique runs. Valentina does nothing.

Run.

VALENTINA
Why?

MONIQUE
Run after me!

VALENTINA
Why.

MONIQUE
To catch me!

VALENTINA
Why?

MONIQUE
You won't know until you do it!

Valentina runs after Monique. Monique turns back catches Valentina.
They look at each other a spell.
Monique puts Valentina's hand on her waist. They dance. Something old and slow from another time but like they just discovered it.

Remember that?

VALENTINA
This?

MONIQUE
Remember when this was just this. Nothing else but just.

VALENTINA
Yes. I remember. No. I don't remember. Was this before?

MONIQUE
Yes. It was before.
Before we'd ever even been in a club.
Or on a plane.
Out of the neighborhood even!
Before the shootings
Before The D/

VALENTINA
/Don't. Say it.

MONIQUE
Before you
You remember now?
In my room when my mother thought we were having a sleepover. Well, it was a sleep over, just not the kind of sleepover she thought we were having!

Laughter.

VALENTINA
Yes, Before

MONIQUE
And After. The next day when I saw you in the cafeteria. And everything was different?

VALENTINA
Yes.

MONIQUE
We had

VALENTINA
/Yes.

MONIQUE
A secret.

VALENTINA
/Yes.

MONIQUE
That was just ours.

VALENTINA.
That was a different before. Different than this before. Remember when it was always just before? Before before before?

MONIQUE
Yes, I remember.

VALENTINA
What are we going to do?

MONIQUE
We are going to be just like before. Even though it is After. We are going to do before again. We are not going to let them take before away from us.

VALENTINA
Before. Forever.

She spits on her hand and holds it up.

MONIQUE
Yes.
Forever.

Monique spits on her hand and presses it into Valentina's hand.

We aren't going to let After stop us. From anything.

VALENTINA
From. Anything.

MONIQUE
From. Love.

VALENTINA
(Beat.) No. We aren't.

MONIQUE

We aren't.

They slow dance. They lean into each other so deeply.
Valentina disappears. Monique looks around at the world.
She looks at the audience. She knows they are looking at
her.

Everyone is watching everything. Everywhere.
She knows that.
She wonders if it's possible to go back to before.
No one knows.

> End of play

LIGHT

by dave solomon

dave solomon is an award-winning Brooklyn-based writer and director working in both theatre and film. He is grateful to have been a part of this project and you can find out more about him and his other work here: www.dave-solomon.com/bio

Contact: Michael Finkle / WME

MFinkle@wmeentertainment.com

212.903.1144

Darkness. An empty space.

Music fades in. Dance / R&B. A heavy beat. A reasonable volume...loud, but not *too* loud.

Lights creep in...and start to strobe and swirl. Colors fill the room.

The space and stage transforming into a dance floor.

We sit in the music and light for a few moments.

A somewhat distant gunshot is heard.

Then another.

Two people enter; they are dancing.

The music gets a bit louder.

The two people are *in* the music – dancing, moving, feeling every beat – we see them both in shadow and light as they move through the space...smiling, never stopping...dancing together and apart...

The music builds.

A round of automatic gunfire rings out...louder now, closer. The dancers are unaffected, they don't hear it...they just keep dancing. More people enter the room...also dancing...filling up the floor. They are moving amongst each other and with each other...

The music gets louder. The lights brighter.

More gunfire. The music grows even LOUDER...as if it were intentionally rising to drown out the shots. More people dance into the space, joining the others. Everyone in the room is still smiling...living and loving...unaffected...hearing only the music and feeling the dance.

More gunshots. Music rises...even more people join the dance floor. The lights are getting brighter and brighter....the white light starting to drown out the colors....and growing out of the colors...

Even more gunshots...a steady, almost endless automatic stream of fire that the music counters, building above it and finally drowning it out completely as the dance floor is now filled with forty-nine dancing bodies of all shapes, sizes and colors!

The light builds and builds until the bright white light and steady jubilant beat and bass completely overtake the room...

Dance. Joy. Love. Everything and everybody aglow... until we are encompassed and almost blinded by bright, white light. The music crescendos! The dancers rise up and let loose in gestures of triumph and exhilaration as the lights snap to black.

Silence. Darkness....with a glow.

STROBOSCOPE

(or Dancing in slow motion)

by Saviana Stanescu

Saviana Stanescu is an award-winning Romanian-American playwright and poet based in Ithaca, NY. Winner of New York Innovative Theatre Award and Best Romanian Play of the Year. Her works include *Aliens with Extraordinary Skills, Ants, White Embers, Useless, Toys, For a Barbarian Woman, Waxing West,* and *Zebra 2.0*. She is an Associate Professor and Chair of Theatre Studies at Ithaca College.

Representation:

Elaine Devlin Literary, Inc.

1115 Broadway, 12th floor, New York, NY 10010

(212) 842-9030 - elaine@edevlinlit.com

MIRA - 30/40s, female, Latina

FAB - 20s, female, black (FAB is written on the front of her T-Shirt)

KOOL - 19, male, any race/ethnicity (KOOL is written on the back of his T-Shirt)

/ - point of overlapping lines

A club, late at night. Loud music. People are dancing.

Mira notices Fab, who's dancing not too far (but not too close) from her.

MIRA *(in her mind)*:

Cute. And sexy. Is she smiling at me, or--?

FAB *(in her mind, about Mira)*:

That hot mama is starring at me...

MIRA *(in her mind)*

Ay mamí tù tan caliente... Did I say that aloud? Can't even hear myself, this crazy music---

KOOL *(to Fab, about Mira)*:

Someone is like / totally starring at you

FAB *(can't hear him first)*: Huh?! Oh, I know...

MIRA *(in her mind)*:

What am I doing here, I'm too old for clubbing...

KOOL *(to Fab)*:

Go say hellooo...

FAB

Nah... She's gotta come to me--

MIRA *(in her mind)*

Fuck it, I'm not too old! Caramba!

KOOL *(to Fab)*

What?! Can't hear you!

FAB

That guy has an eye on you!

KOOL

Which one?!

FAB

I dunno, find one! It's like I'm here with my little brother.

Stroboscope light. Letters on T-shirts are glowing.

MIRA *(in her mind)*

Ha. FAB - of course. Your T-shirt doesn't lie, girl. But who's that 'kool' guy talking to you? Kool and Fab-- Are they a couple? No, he's just a friend, he's--- Is he-- ?

FAB *(dancing in Mira's direction, in her mind)*

C'mon, mami. Don't be afraid, I don't bite. Or maybe I do-- And maybe you like it---

MIRA *(in her mind)*

Is she-- kinda---? She is.

Mira starts dancing her way towards Fab.

KOOL *(to Fab)*

Gonna get a drink... Want / something?

FAB

Wow. She's totally coming. / *(to Kool)* Go!

KOOL

Who?! *(noticing Mira approaching)* Someone is gonna have fun tonite---

Mira gets closer, dancing. Fab dances towards Mira as well.

Gun shots. They go unnoticed for a while due to the loud music.

Mia and Fab are immersed in their dance towards each other.

Kool realizes what's happening - a shooter! - he's paralyzed for a moment.

KOOL

Fuck!

Mira and Fab are now very close to each other, they can't hear Kool.

MIRA

Hey, *(pointing at the glowing letters on Fab's chest)* FAB...

FAB

Hey--

They smile at each other.

KOOL

(running towards Fab) Shooter! Run!

Gun shot noises get louder/closer. Glowing light.

Mira, Fab and Kool get shot. They fall down in slow motion, looking at each other, surprised, not fully understanding what's happening to them.

Mira manages to grab Fab's hand while falling, they reach the floor hand in hand.

Blackout.

CLAIM

By Ken Urban

Ken Urban is a playwright and screenwriter. Recent plays include *A Guide For The Homesick* (Huntington Theatre Company, West End), *The Remains* (Studio Theatre), *Sense of an Ending* (59E59 Theatres, London's Theatre503), and *Nibbler* (The Amoralists). Awards include Weissberger Playwriting Award, New York Foundation for the Arts Fellowship, Dramatist Guild Fellowship, and MacDowell Colony Fellowships. Ken is a resident playwright at New Dramatists and affiliated writer at the Playwrights' Center. He wrote the screenplay for the feature film *The Happy Sad*, directed by Rodney Evans. He leads the band Occurrence.

For rights to this piece:

Luke Virkstis, WME. LVirkstis@wmeagency.com. 1 212 903-1100

CHARACTERS

CARLOS

MOTHER

TODD

NARRATOR

**

CARLOS
Would you claim my body?

NARRATOR
Carlos has just called his mother. They haven't spoken in the decade since he came out.

CARLOS
Would you claim my body?

MOTHER
What kind of question is that?

NARRATOR
The unnamed Puerto Rican man, the 49th victim shot in that club in Orlando, his father disowned him, refusing to claim his body.

CARLOS
Would you do that if I was one of the dead?

MOTHER
This terrible thing happens and you make it about yourself.

CARLOS
Answer the question.

MOTHER
All the terrible violence of this summer, and you remember that one detail.

CARLOS
I could've have been there.

MOTHER
You live in Pittsburgh.

CARLOS
Mom, I've gone on vacation to Florida.

MOTHER
Why? Florida is a terrible place. Full of crazies and terrorists.

CARLOS
That man wasn't a terrorist. Or he was... I don't know.

MOTHER
That sad man who shot up all those people at the club wasn't a terrorist?

CARLOS
Not in the way you mean.

MOTHER
A lot of brown people in this world shooting up places and murdering people.

CARLOS
We're Brown People, Mami.

TODD
Why did you even call her?

NARRATOR
Later, when he was with Todd.

TODD
Why call her? What did you expect her to say?

CARLOS
I don't know.

TODD
Why do you need her to apologize so much?

CARLOS
To recognize that her attitude, it's the same attitude… that leads to that shooting.

TODD
I'm trying to suck your dick. And you're ruining the mood.

NARRATOR
It was true. Todd was trying to get Carlos off before bed, and this subject was not conducive to anyone's erection.

TODD
Now. Focus.

CARLOS
Would you claim my body?

MOTHER
Again with this question, Carlos.

NARRATOR
That same night, Carlos had called her again, Todd asleep at his side.

MOTHER
Why does it matter so much?

CARLOS
I'm in bed with a man I love.

MOTHER
Your mother is alone, watching *Law & Order* re-runs.

CARLOS
Do you think I'm really worth nothing because I'm gay?

MOTHER
I would grieve you. That is all I can say.

CARLOS
What does that mean? "I would grieve you."

NARRATOR
The next morning.

TODD
You want your mom to say she'll claim your body. Maybe she would. Maybe she wouldn't. It doesn't change the fact there are people in this world that fucking hate us. Would you have even told her you were gay ten years ago if she hadn't caught you with that neighbor?

CARLOS
Course, I would've.

TODD
If your dad were still alive? Would you have told him?

CARLOS
I-I-I don't know.

NARRATOR
An answer that will sit with them both for a long time, Carlos thinking about all the times that Todd wanted to take his hand and Carlos thought:

CARLOS
Not here.

NARRATOR

All the times, he thought to himself

CARLOS

I don't need to correct my co-workers' assumption I got a girl.

NARRATOR

And all of that sits with him, still no answer to that question:

CARLOS

Would you claim my body?

***

NoPassport Press was founded in 2003 by playwright Caridad Svich. It is devoted to the publication of new writing for performance, theatrical works in translation, and curated theatre actions for social justice. It publishes on the Lulu Books print on demand platform.

www.ingramcontent.com/pod-product-compliance
Lightning Source LLC
LaVergne TN
LVHW020356090825
818278LV00039B/1058